Years on Air

I Huw

TELERI BEVAN
Years on Air

y Lolfa

ISBN: 0 86243 717 2

Printed and published in Wales
by Y Lolfa Cyf., Talybont, Ceredigion SY24 5AP
e-mail ylolfa@ylolfa.com
website www.ylolfa.com
tel. (01970) 832 304
fax 832 782

Acknowledgements

It is almost ten years since the publication of *Years of My Time*, a collection of reminiscences of my upbringing on a farm in Cardiganshire. That story ended at a particular turning point in my life, with the beginning of a new career in broadcasting.

Years on Air tells of the ups and downs during those decades with BBC Wales, and it is now thirteen years since I retired: time for memories to mature like good wine. I have been fortunate whilst drafting this book in that two former colleagues, Gareth Price and John Stuart Roberts, read the first manuscript, and their comments on structure and narrative were enormously helpful; two close friends, Sheila Cross and Enid Wilkinson, were always, always encouraging and supportive, and Peter Day, who has spent a lifetime in publishing, was incisive in analysis, yet kind and thoughtful as he set about correcting and editing. But the real back-up came from my family, young and old.

Diolch iddyn nhw, bob un. Ac hefyd i wasg Y Lolfa am eu caredigrwydd, ac i'r Cyngor Llyfrau am gefnogi'r gyfrol.

Preface

I was eight when I decided I wanted to be a Master of Foxhounds just like Lady Pryse, owner of the Gogerddan Hunt. Every week, I joined her to ride the byways of the countryside north of Aberystwyth, through copses and woodlands, in search of foxes daft enough to be active on Saturday mornings in mid-winter. It was wartime and my involvement began in October 1939, a month after Prime Minister Chamberlain had declared war against Hitler and the Nazi regime. There was no connection between the two events; I was not a bloodthirsty bully, but my parents had long realised that I was a rebellious child, the middle one of three sisters. They bought me a black Welsh mountain pony and, at a stroke, gave me the wonderful gift of freedom to roam. Every Saturday, at nine o'clock in the morning, Bess and I, groomed and polished, set out on our own towards Gogerddan mansion, a mile away, to meet Lady Pryse and her motley pack of hounds. She was a leader and I was a follower. She was a lady apart, trim and sedate, dressed in the livery of her position, crimson jacket, hairnet to keep her steel-grey hair in position, hard, black peaked hat pulled down to the eyebrows, white breeches and long, black boots, she rode her grey mare, Mary, as to the manor born, straight backed and composed.

She said very little, her morning greeting to me, as she caught sight of me waiting in the stable courtyard, was, 'Teleri,' coupled with a touch of the whip to the brim of her cap before mounting, ready for the off. Little was said for the next four or five hours, but people and dogs obeyed her softly spoken commands without question. When a hound picked up a fox's scent, its long howl of excitement caused solemn and dignified Lady Pryse to change personality, to become a different lady. She clutched the golden hunting horn to her lips and blew until her face turned bright purple, her body tightened and twitched with aggression, but foxes in this part of the world were free spirits, not oppressed or chastened, and I have no recollection in eight years as a follower, of a fox being killed 'on the run'. They were never long-drawn-out affairs; the aged hounds often lost the trail but, oddly, she rarely showed any sign of irritation or anger. It was a game, a piece of theatre, with Lady Pryse, dressed for the part in red and white, taking the starring role against the backdrop of glorious Cardiganshire countryside. I loved it and I wanted to dress and be like her.

Four years later, I had succumbed to other influences. I had reached another certainty. I wanted to be a film star. The romance of the Hollywood dream factory and the glamorous lifestyle of the stars invoked magic and enchantment. I was hooked. There were three cinemas in Aberystwyth; twice a week, I went to the pictures and paid my three pence to sit on a bench in the gods, almost touching the roof of the Coliseum film palace. I read every magazine on the lifestyle of the stars: Clark Gable, Alan Ladd, Van Johnson, Gary Cooper, Hedy Lamaar, Joan Crawford, Greer Garson, Katherine Hepburn and others. I knew them all. I admired them. I wanted to be like them, in their world of make-believe. If only a talent scout would choose me to act, to be someone else, then, at a stroke, I would be transported to another world. Living in Aberystwyth during the war years, an ocean away from Hollywood, we needed dreams. There was little glamour about and, too often, romance turned into raw lust. When I saw the film *National Velvet*, with Elizabeth Taylor, who was roughly my age, in the starring role, I believed everything was possible. I had a pony, I was a country girl and a farmer's daughter, but any similarity with Elizabeth Taylor, pushing herself to glorious victory on her pony in the Grand National, ended just there. I was nothing like her, but in my dreams I ached for someone to discover me and make me a star.

Sometime around the age of sixteen, reality hit hard, the vivid Technicolor dreams turned dull sepia. At school, I failed a crucial matriculation examination, and I broke a leg, which kept me in bed for four months. I was on the brink of being an abject failure, not interested in schoolwork and not concerned about a future career. I was a bit of a tomboy (how I hated that word) and yet, in my dreams, I remained starry-eyed, wanting to be an actress. It was not a dream I shared with anyone, not even with my sisters, but during the long, freezing winter of 1947, the time for realism and making hard choices was forced upon me. My parents had been fortunate members of their respective families who had benefited from university and teacher training college education. They impressed on us that education brought freedom and independence. Failure meant you tried again and, if necessary, you tried repeatedly. Driven by this work ethic, I managed to gain a place at the University College of North Wales, Bangor, and there I followed a rural science degree course in botany and agricultural botany and, in the final year, I studied animal nutrition.

However, I never once lost sight of that other goal: to be a star, or, as the years passed, to be a part of the entertainment business. During schooldays, I satisfied my aspiration with minor roles in drama productions. I found work with the local professional repertory company, led by Alexander and Edna Dore, based in a makeshift theatre in Bath Street, brushing the stage, making cups of tea and helping in the box office. The smell of the greasepaint and the sound of applause were like an aphrodisiac. At university, I took a step closer, acting in and directing revues and musical extravaganzas, but no agent or talent scout plucked me from obscurity to set me on the course to stardom. It was a bleak prospect. I needed a proper job and eventually I found myself in East Anglia as the Organiser of Young Farmers' Clubs for the Isle of Ely and the county of Cambridgeshire. If the outlook was bleak, the flat, grey landscape held little enchantment compared with the hills of west Wales, but the fenland people were friendly, hospitable and tough. The city of Ely became my home for eighteen months, but a chance glimpse through the *Daily Telegraph*, one misty autumn morning, when I was in a doctor's waiting room, galvanised me into action. My eyes had focused on an advertisement for an assistant radio producer at the BBC in Cardiff. I knew very little about radio other than as a listener, even less about the structures of the BBC, but I knew enough to realise that this was a chance to get a toehold in the entertainment business. I read the advertisement twenty times. The job, if I was successful, meant a salary of £645 a year, an increase of £245 on my income at that time. It entailed assisting the work of producers in the Children's Hour department in Cardiff, producing radio programmes in Welsh and English for the Welsh Home Service. I had no experience of working with children, although, as I told myself when my application form disappeared into the post-box, a few young farmers were very young indeed.

I waited and waited for a reply, and eventually, six weeks later, I received an invitation to attend an interview in London. It was to be my first contact with the formality of the BBC's bureaucratic structure. The process turned out to be thorough and lengthy, taking almost five months in total. The letter said this was to be a preliminary interview with the senior appointments officer based at the Langham, Portland Place. The authenticity of my application – Welsh speaker – fenland – rural affairs background – must have intrigued the departmental system; my credentials needed to be checked and verified before I could be let loose in Cardiff. The gentleman interviewer, a Mr Ramsay, thin, pin-striped, grey and languid, sat behind his desk. He made me welcome and then asked a few questions, as he struggled with the peel of a blood orange, and I saw the juice cascade over my application form.

'It'll be a matter for Wales to make a decision,' he said eventually, wiping his hands on a bright blue handkerchief. 'I'll pass the information on to them.'

I felt as though I had discovered the mysterious competition character, Lobby Lud, from the *News Chronicle*. Mr Ramsay seemed relieved, even surprised, at his own decisiveness. Six weeks later, I found myself facing a formal interviewing panel of four dark-suited gentlemen at Broadcasting House, Cardiff. I was nervous beforehand, but I believed I had conducted myself reasonably well, shown enough feminine guile to convince the panel that I was worldly-wise, enthusiastic and creative. I had obeyed my mother's instruction to the letter: 'Sit up straight, look tidy and think before you speak.'

Following half an hour of questioning, the Chairman interrupted his doodling on the papers in front of him, to call the interview to a close.

Suddenly, a voice from the end of the table boomed, 'One last question, if I may, please, Mr Chairman.' The man looked directly at me. 'Producing programmes means working in a team. 'Tell me…' and at this point he twirled a pencil between his stubby fingers. 'Tell me, how will you get on with men?'

His attitude was so blatantly sexist, and one I was to meet several times during the next decades. I paused. Images of canoodling at school, torrid affairs at university, and coping with the raw appetite of young farmers for flirting and haystacks flashed through my mind. Somehow, I stumbled out my reply. 'How will they get on with me?'

The pencil went into overdrive, and the dark grey, serge suit bulged with power.

'We will decide that,' the Chairman declared; which concluded the interview, and I was ushered out of the room.

I was not an outraged feminist but I could, if pushed, set a match to the odd bra. For the first time, that question had made me realise that men and women were 'equal but different'. It took the board another two months of deliberation before writing to offer me the job.

Thus, I became a member of BBC staff in Wales on St. David's Day, 1955, and I was to spend almost four decades working in public service broadcasting, an occupation that excited, enthralled, fulfilled and occasionally irritated me. In these years of immense change, there were to be achievements and failures; occasionally, prejudice and bias; and there were colleagues and friends. The growth and development in the communications industry has had a profound effect on people's lives and thinking. The digital revolution, satellite and technological advances mean that today, at the touch of a button, we are able to communicate with communities in all parts of the globe. In 1955, the broadcasting fraternity was striving to hold together the old structured order, and there were obvious signs of tensions, in particular linguistic ones. Very many listeners felt the programme output of the Welsh Home Service favoured the Welsh language. 'The tail wagging the dog,' as Ian Jacob, the Director General, wrote to one protestor. The BBC at that time was one national institution, hierarchical and controlled by London, where lofty directors referred to all broadcasting establishments outside the headquarters in London as regions, or provincial production centres.

I was to enter a close-knit community. Radio was the dominant medium; television was in its infancy, with an output of seven programmes a month, using a cumbersome outside broadcast unit. The staff had come from working in radio, and the battle had begun between those who believed in the power of the screen image, and those who believed in the image created by words. In 1955, the pompously named department of the Spoken Word was abolished, and, significantly, the BBC's monopoly was broken with the reality of commercial television. The growing popularity of television reshaped traditional views of culture and society. The years of post-war austerity and rationing had gone, society was becoming more consumer-orientated, and Prime Minister Harold Macmillan was about to tell us, 'We have never had it so good.' Churches and chapels were striving to come to terms with a new youth culture, and I remember well the impact of the film,

Rock Around the Clock, when it came to Cardiff's Capitol Cinema, and we rocked up Park Place, with the heavy beat and rhythm of Bill Haley and his Comets resounding around us.

One of the pleasures of retirement is having the time to contemplate and to recall – not that I have sunk into a well of nostalgia – and it would be folly to attempt to chronicle the achievements and failures of the BBC during those years. For most of the time, I was a producer and, occasionally, a presenter of programmes. Then, in the last decade of my working life, I became an editor and a manager. I do not intend to compare today's activities with those of my day, which was yesterday. It is not an assessment either. It is a collection of retrospective glimpses of people and events as I recollect them, and as they affected me.

I trust the passage of time has not blunted my powers of objectivity. For me, BBC staff number 57672, the past was rich in character and incident.

The Fifties

One

That first morning, walking up the steps of Broadcasting House, I felt anticipation and nervousness. In my mind, this was the big time, the entertainment business, and I was dressed in my one and only best suit, a rather formal, cherry red, Hebe pleated skirt and jacket. I was taken immediately to the canteen, which I soon realised was the daily meeting place. The glitterati of Welsh broadcasting gathered there for their morning cup of tea, and discussion of the day's gossip and happenings. I looked around; they were not quite my notion of glamorous show-business types. Men with flat, shining, Brylcreemed hair wore sober, three-piece suits, and women were in their ensembles of the day: classical skirts and twin sets, or demure blouses. This was the era when so many prominent broadcasters in Wales were sons and daughters of the manse. They were regarded as people of 'quality', of probity and high morals, possessed of extra vocal gifts, language and confidence for the microphone. I sat quietly, listening to the gossip, which, on that patronal day, focused on a live radio transmission of a grand celebratory concert that was to be broadcast that evening from the Sophia Gardens pavilion.

A voice whispered in my left ear, 'Where do you come from?'

I turned to look at a distinguished, grey-haired, red-faced, twinkling-eyed gentleman. I replied, 'Aberystwyth.'

I could almost feel him thinking that I must be one of those loose Welsh Nationalists from west Wales. His curiosity now aroused, he asked, 'What have you been doing before coming to the BBC?'

I told him I had been the organiser for Young Farmers' Clubs in the Isle of Ely and Cambridge. His bushy eyebrows shot up to the grey hairline, the blue eyes narrowed, and he asked the only question that seems to matter to Welsh men and women.

'What does your father do?'

I answered, 'He's a farmer.'

His cup of tea clattered down on the saucer and he smiled his surprise. 'Good God! How did you get in here?'

I have yet to find a satisfactory answer. The perceptive gentleman was not the son of the manse but someone well known for his abrasive style and sharp wit. He was Rae Jenkins, conductor of the BBC Welsh Orchestra, and he became a good friend. During the war years, he was well known to millions of listeners as conductor of the Variety Orchestra and for his role in the popular series *ITMA*, when the inimitable Tommy Handley would instruct him, 'Play, Rae.' He taught me, an ignoramus as far as music was concerned, how to appreciate and understand the works of great composers. I had never been to an orchestral concert before joining the BBC, and those first months working with Rae, and composer and musician Mansel Thomas, making music programmes for children, were pivotal to my education. During his student days, Mansel, who was at that time Head of Music, had been organist at one of the great London Welsh Methodist Chapels, Shirland Road, where my Aunty Lizzie was a member. Whenever I met her, her countenance softened, to take on the look of someone who had worshipped from afar, and she would ask gently, 'Seen Mansel lately?'

So began my life in broadcasting and with the BBC in Wales. At twenty-three, I was the youngest staff producer and, according to Watkin Jones, the Head of Programmes, mine was likely to be the last radio production appointment, given the rapid growth and dominance of television. I was to work with Lorraine Davies in the *Children's Hour* department. She produced and organised, with her deputy, Evelyn Williams, who was based at the Bangor production centre in north Wales, an hour and a half of Welsh-language radio programmes a week. They were broadcast weekly between 5 and 6 p.m. on Tuesdays and 5.30 and 6 p.m. on Thursdays. In addition, they produced English programmes on a regular basis for the network's *Children's Hour* service. It was a busy, demanding schedule, and both women were creative, skilled practitioners in a wide range of programming, from story telling, serials and single plays to music-making, outside broadcasts and quizzes. I was to be the new assistant, although Lorraine, as the *Children's Hour* Organiser, had not been a member of the interviewing panel. I met her for the first time on my first working day, and, within minutes, I knew this formidable lady was not going to give me an easy ride.

I was assigned a desk in the corner of her office, under the eaves of Broadcasting House, Cardiff. It was a building adapted from three large, grey-stoned villas in Park Place, opposite the National Museum of Wales. It contained office accommodation, four radio studios, a technical communications department, a newsroom and a small canteen. Lorraine's secretary, Joan Jenkins, another formidable, no nonsense lady, occupied the third corner of our third floor office. Whether by accident or design, both had been brought up in the same village, Glyn Neath, in the Neath valley, and at times, as the *Children's Hour* live transmission deadline of five o'clock approached, after a day-long rehearsal, the give and take between the two could be volcanic. Lorraine's demands reached a high crescendo in those last minutes before a broadcast: another packet of cigarettes, a jug of water, a page missing from a script; and Joan, who always worked nine to five office hours, would make a final appeal for an answer to one of her pressing problems.

'I've got London on the line; they need an answer today about the concert tomorrow.'

'They'll have to wait.'

'They can't. They need to know now.'

Lorraine's commands were to be obeyed without question, but Joan's mutterings, as she closed the studio door after another unsuccessful mission, were always threatening. 'She'll come to a sticky end,' was the most notable.

Lorraine was stylish, disciplined and organised, renowned for her editorial judgement and script analysis, her production skills recognised instantly to be of the highest quality and standard. That first week, I watched her in action during rehearsals of an adventure drama. She was like a power dynamo. Short, dark-haired, she sat on the edge of her studio chair, her expressive brown eyes fixed on the script, flicking ash from a cigarette every ten seconds, issuing instructions crisply, and castigating mistakes and fluffs promptly. Not for one moment did she lose concentration, and woe betide anyone who did. Her face stern and resolute, she could erupt like a firecracker but only because she demanded the best from everyone. She was also the child of her valley. Outwardly tough and courageous, she was also warm, open, and all heart.

Lorraine was married to Hywel Davies, the Assistant Head of Programmes. They made a formidable partnership in their crowded and demanding life. He was a complete broadcaster who was becoming a visionary programme administrator. The broadcasting fraternity was fascinated with their lifestyle, often tempestuous, full of incident, but generous and stylish.

The outward preoccupation with her work and a colourful persona hid a more vulnerable aspect of Lorraine's character. I remember one sunny Friday afternoon when she let her defences come tumbling down as she recalled the horror of the day when a wartime bomb destroyed her first marriage. The house was completely demolished during the first bombing raid on the city of York. Her husband, Noel Jameson, died instantly, and Lorraine was entombed in the rubble for twenty-four hours while she waited to be rescued. She spent weeks in hospital, and returned home to Neath to recover from the trauma, eventually to resume her teaching career. The memory of those events occasionally bubbled to the surface, and her normally vivacious manner would become morose and questioning; that outward show of cool poise crumbling into uncertainty.

During my first months of learning, she was awesome and fearsome, and I soon realised it would take me until my retirement to reach her high standards. Despite going to London to attend a six-week training course in radio production, the Lorraine teachings were the make or break ones. Sitting at my desk in the office, waiting for her morning entrance, I knew her comments on my production and presentation effort the previous evening would be pithy and to the point. 'Competent' was her most damning comment. In her eyes, I had not tried hard enough; but one significant lesson that I learned in those early days was to be direct and honest in appraisal. Lorraine could criticise and dissect decisively and objectively. Without equivocation, she could also praise generously and warmly.

The BBC of those days was administered by high-minded gentlemen, who tended to see only the glories of the past, especially the war years. They clung obstinately to the complexity and inflexibility of the structure, and I learned the hard way. Taking criticism from my peers was almost a way of life, as was coming to terms with the notion that all my mistakes were public ones. There were strange customs and protocols within the operational system, and there were acronyms, hundreds of them. They symbolised a sophisticated bureaucracy. On paper and in meetings, Controller Wales was always addressed as CW. Similarly, the post of Head of Programmes became HPW, and one senior executive from the engineering division was famously known as EIEIO. During my first week, Lorraine asked me to find a P as B. I spent some hours searching offices and asking, 'Have you seen a P as B?' until a kind soul told me to look in a filing cabinet. It was a document called Programme as Broadcast.

There were wonderful compensations and experiences too, as I grew to know the people, absorbed the atmosphere, and came to realise that live programmes were ephemeral. Today's disaster could turn into tomorrow's hope. The daily *Children's Hour* range and quality of programme-making was a joy, but few recordings of those years remain today. There are scripts in a variety of forms in archive libraries, but they do not have the resonance of the spoken word, or of the total action.

The first few months gave me an excellent opportunity to watch distinguished radio producers at work. Elwyn Evans was a master at producing and directing dramatic features, with large casts, for live, two-hour, evening transmissions. Many actors were familiar voices, members of the BBC's Repertory Company. They were on the books not merely for their talent, but for their range and versatility in Welsh and English. They included former Rhondda miners, craggy-voiced Prysor Williams and Moses Jones; the childlike voice of Olive Michael; the vocal authority of the archetypal Welsh Mam, Rachel Thomas; and the silken sexiness of Ennis Tinnusche. Plays on a range of themes tested every possible emotion, and many actors such as Dillwyn Owen, Brinley Jenkins, Norman Wynne, Dilys Davies and Gwenyth Petty were often cast to take on a mix of roles in one production. There were other regulars, too, who adorned the radio-acting scene, but who earned their living in other occupations. John Darran, Peter and Arthur Phillips were solicitors, and Wyn Thomas was an architect. They were all familiar voices to listeners of the Welsh Home Service in the '50s, and as a new recruit to production, I knew I would have to depend on their goodwill and understanding in the future.

Perhaps the greatest thrill of all was meeting and seeing at work the legendary producer, Mai Jones. During the post-war years, she created what proved to be one of the most popular radio variety series of the time, *Welsh Rarebit*, but I guess her most lasting legacy is her composition of the haunting song, *We'll Keep a Welcome*. Gifted as a musician, accompanist and composer, she had an acute sense of entertainment and audience. She knew show business, and she knew what appealed, and was unashamedly an emotional and nostalgic populist. She had experienced the vicissitudes of performing in music halls, in vaudeville and on concert platforms, and she knew what elements made a successful variety show. 'Booking the right acts and working out the right order,' was the principle she brought from the theatre to radio variety. Her reputation for giving new talent such as Harry Secombe, Shirley Bassey, Gladys Morgan, Geraint Evans and Bruce Dargavel their first opportunity has been widely recognised, as was her ability to give a Welsh dimension to all her compositions, arrangements and musical productions.

In my book, Mai Jones epitomised show business, and although the glamorous life and hard work had taken its toll and she was close to retirement when I first met her, even so, when she walked into a room, she seemed to take centre stage. Tall, blonde, heavily made-up, with full, bright, pillar-box-red lipstick on her lips, she was every inch a show-biz theatrical person; dressed in pastel-coloured gowns and wide-brimmed hats, it always seemed to me as if she was prepared for her next performance. At the mandatory Monday afternoon meetings, chaired by Hywel Davies, when studios were allocated to producers and their productions, Mai would glide through the door, late, apologetic, fluttering gently like a pale-coloured butterfly caught in a summer breeze, after a prolonged lunchtime visit to the Overseas Club, next door to Broadcasting House.

With impeccable timing, she would arrive just in time to hear Hywel Davies ask, 'Any bids for the Cory Hall?' and since she was the only producer to use the great temperance hall on a regular basis, for the production of *Welsh Rarebit*, the request was agreed on a nod. It was her only programme commitment for the week. That business done, she would get up slowly from her chair, clutching the brim of her hat, to leave as she came in, swaying with the panache of a seasoned performer who had devised the Queen Mother look before Her Majesty went on to perfect it.

Two

In September 1955, I was given my very own series of radio programmes to produce. It was to be a year-long series of outside broadcasts, and although I had listened to erudite lectures from talk and drama practitioners during the training course in London, no-one had really explained the technique of mounting an outside broadcast and how best to maintain continuity of action between different scenes and locations. The series of twelve half-hour programmes spanned a year in the life of Gelli Aur, the farm institute in Carmarthenshire, a training college for students, mainly sons and daughters of farmers, housed in a beautiful old manor house in the Tywi valley. Lorraine believed this would test my ability as a producer, and demonstrate whether I could organise effectively the necessary technical resources and, more important, whether I could create an entertaining and an informative programme for children aged between eight and twelve. At a stroke, she would know whether the interviewing board had recruited an asset to her department.

The series was not a total disaster but the early episodes came close to being my meltdown. As I now recall with embarrassment, the first three programmes were dominated by the clinking sound of measured footsteps on tarmacadam, when the presenters, Llywelyn Phillips and Ann Morgan, were heard to move from scene to scene. It was a walking disaster of confused continuity and entangled logistics, as much of the action was taking place on open, grassy fields.

In accordance with practice, the programme content, its script of narrative and dialogue, was committed to paper, back in the office, a week or so before the recording took place on location. In my mind, my imagination ran riot; sitting at my desk under the eaves, I aimed for realism and atmosphere. Without fully understanding the severe limitations of the technology at my disposal, I envisaged that the action would move seamlessly from scene to scene, from location to location. We rehearsed on location, read and timed each scene accurately, occasionally adding a 'Well' here, and an 'Um' there, in an attempt to make our contributors appear and sound as natural as possible. They were mainly farmhands, or youthful students, who had never been involved in such epics, and often spoke their lines as though they were in chapel on Sunday morning, intoning verses from the New Testament.

It was a slow process. The era of tape and flexibility had not yet dawned in Wales. The material was recorded in blocks of four minutes, cut onto a disc by a recording machine that was carried in the boot of a majestic, black Rover car. The microphone cables did not allow contributors to walk and talk for more than six paces. A scene running to more than four minutes was enough to give Fred, the engineer, stress spasms as the cutting needle wobbled uncontrollably when the disc became full. But the spasms during the location recording were as nothing compared to those experienced by studio managers back in the studio at Broadcasting House. Their job was to unravel continuity problems from the heap of fragile discs, which they could only play once, at most twice, for rehearsal purposes. To make matters worse, it was almost impossible to cut or edit the material. Only the most skilled operator would venture 'jump cuts' during live transmissions. It was an operation calling for dexterity, timing and bravery, to lift the needle from the turntable at a designated 'out point' word, move the needle arm in a split second above a marked spot, and drop the needle on the 'in point' word, with a disc spinning at 78 r.p.m. Not every studio manager was practised in such delicate manoeuvrings; one or two had to lie down with a cold compress on their foreheads after fraught hiatuses in an 'up to the minute', unrehearsed news programme.

My series was transmitted at 5.25 p.m. on Thursday afternoon, and the studio manager who was allocated to me in Studio 4 liked the *Overseas Club* liquid lunches. Because I was new and inexperienced, and because Dai's bonhomie level was always at an all-time high after lunch, he suggested during rehearsal, that if we encountered problems or difficulty with continuity, such as unforced gaps, we could fill them with the sound of footsteps taken from the 'discs effects library.' His experience was encouraging.

'I can fade in the footsteps when we hit a gap, or a problem.' He paused dramatically before he explained, 'We won't have gaps, then, you see.'

Gaps, or silences, of more than ten seconds on air could initiate the emergency procedure in the communications department, where engineers monitored every transmission. A disc of Bow Bells was always on standby, and their peals, caused by programme under-runs, or breakdowns, often punctuated a day's listening.

Several problems surfaced one particular Thursday. The speed lever on the effects disc turntable moved erratically, and listeners were treated to the sound of Llewelyn's feet bursting into a Goon-type race somewhere between the pigsty and the silo pit. The programme never recovered from these flying footsteps, and it prompted Hywel Davies, as the Assistant Head of Programmes, the man in charge of output, to ring the studio in anger.

'That was the worst programme I've heard this year.'

It was the December edition and my third programme. I survived, as did the series, and I completed the run of twelve.

I was launched on a perpendicular learning process. Working with composer Grace Williams was an enriching experience, when she adapted and compiled a series of informative and entertaining programmes on works such as *L'Enfance du Christ* and Ravel's *L'Enfant et les Sortilèges*. She could appear detached and aloof, exact and precise, but she was an enthusiast, and kindling the interest of children in classical music gave her enormous pleasure. Music programmes were a special joy, and to be involved in live music making with the orchestra was instructive. Concerts for children, with Rae Jenkins on the rostrum, were demanding and occasionally hair-raising experiences. The tempo could change from *adagio* to *accelerando* at an agitated wave of his baton, as Rae watched the clock, determined to end the concert on the second before the pips heralded the six o'clock news.

Lorraine ensured that I should be tested in all manner of productions, even risking another series of outside broadcasts to my care. *Bro Mebyd,* presented by Ifor Rees, gave schoolchildren from all parts of Wales an opportunity to talk about their localities and communities, and Alun Williams, the consummate radio broadcaster, chaired a fortnightly general knowledge quiz. Alun was skilled as a commentator, interviewer, presenter, entertainer and producer. He invited me one evening to accompany him to a recording of his popular light entertainment series, *Shw Mae Heno?*, at Gwauncaegurwen, before an audience consisting of members of a solid Welsh-speaking, coalmining community, where they grew hard men who were sticklers for authority and protocol. I was in deep uncharted waters of prejudice and bias. It became obvious that, in such communities, women knew their place.

During the break between rehearsal and transmission, Alun took me to the local pub, 'to lubricate the tubes'. It was just about opening time. He knocked on the door. *'Wyt ti ar agor nawr?'* he called. (Are you ready to open?) The wooden door rasped over the slate flagstones as it was pulled open to reveal a small, gloomy bar, redolent of stale beer and smoke. We went in. A man greeted Alun warmly. He looked more closely at me, standing against the light.

'Odi honna 'da ti?' (Is she with you?)

'Odi.' (Yes.)

The man propped himself against the bar, his nose almost touching Alun's.

'Gall hi ddim yfed fan hyn.' (She can't drink here.) *'Dim ond dynion.'* (Only men.)

Alun tried again, using all his powers of persuasion, guile and charm. *'O, dere mlan, bachan. Dim ond un bach. Welith neb. Mae'n rhy gynnar.'* (Oh come on. Only a small one. No-one will know. It's too early.)

Nevertheless, nothing would shift him, although he did concede

29

quietly, '*Wy'n lico merched,*' (I like women) and he laughed loudly, winking at me with both eyes.

The radio series *Woman's Hour* did much to change such attitudes. I took over the production of the monthly edition from Wales from Nan Davies. She was a revered talks producer, who began her career in broadcasting as a secretary before the war, but, in 1955, she was appointed Senior Producer and moved from her base at the Bangor production centre to Cardiff. I sought her advice for the first two editions of the programme, and came through the experience unscathed. Her methods were very different from Lorraine's, whose thoughts and ideas were expressed in a direct, somewhat impatient, authoritative manner. Nan would take all the time in the world, patiently cajoling and gently persuading, in an almost conspiratorial manner, as though the next deadline were a week away. Those discussions would invariably conclude with a dig at Lorraine's methods, although they both professed to be the best of friends. Nan liked to think she had a particular and close relationship with the handsome and charming Hywel Davies, but when he married Lorraine, a few years before I arrived at the BBC, Nan gritted her teeth and smiled bravely.

She was knowledgeable and a creative generator of ideas; she knew everyone who was anyone in Wales, and had a great gift for spotting and nurturing talent, mainly young men, I have to admit. Although unmarried and in her late forties, she gave me the impression that young women recruits – and there were not many – were to be tolerated; after all, there was a strong possibility they could undermine things, and worse, become a future threat.

The tightly knit group of female producers who produced

Woman's Hour in London were not in any sense a threat to her. Nan had worked in Wales all her life and had no wish to move to London, although her productions for the Home Service – the Radio 4 of those days – were always distinctively of a high standard. Established in 1946, *Woman's Hour*, as a daily programme, sought initially to reflect the cosy aspect of housekeeping and family life, but sharp editorial policy soon changed that concept, and taboo topics such as the menopause, the use of the pill, and homosexuality were dealt with directly and honestly. Little did I realise, when I began my association with the editorial team in the mid-fifties that I would continue to produce the monthly edition from Wales for the next twenty years. Occasionally, regional programmes broadcast on Friday afternoons at 2 o'clock, as they attempted to reflect aspects and attitudes particular to their areas, were often thought to be editorially too soft, with a tendency to sink into the abyss of parochialism. I remember a short, five-minute talk illustrating the heroic contribution a Welsh nurse from the town of Bala, Betsy Cadwaladr, a contemporary of Florence Nightingale, had made on the battlefields of the Crimean war. It generated some pointed comment, mainly I think because of its title, *From Bala to Balaclava*.

'We applaud and welcome items of universal appeal, but the item you titled *From Bala to Balaclava* was really rather stretching matters, Teleri.' The lofty voice of the then editor, Janet Quigley, at the other end of the telephone made it plain that she was in no mood for excuses. Editors were women of distinction, devoted and formidable – Janet Quigley, Joanna Scott Moncrieff, Monica Sims, Mollie Lee, Wyn Knowles – each in turn was dedicated to the programme. Within half an hour of every broadcast, I would be called to the telephone to hear the editor give detailed comments on the execution of individual items, the programme's overall structure and presentation. Such attention to detail ensured high broadcasting standards and consistency. The programme also built a close relationship with listeners, by taking their comments seriously, and reading their letters on air.

I gathered a small group of regular contributors who, in their turn, gave editions a particular flavour of Wales; they were people who had mastered the art of writing talks for radio. Journalist John Morgan was, at that time, a regular columnist for the *Observer* newspaper, working from his home town of Swansea, who turned to television and became a celebrated reporter on *Panorama*. His insights into and interpretation of our cultural life, and reports on our changing society always provoked a reaction. Harry Soan was much more reflective. His talks evoked images of colours, customs and, occasionally, the cruelty of seasonal life in the countryside, sympathetic thoughts which made him a favourite with listeners. Then, there was Elisabeth Sheppard Jones, whose sense of fun, irreverence and warmth often hid the pain and frustration of her disability. She had been cruelly disabled in the war, when a bomb dropped on the Guards' Chapel in London, where she was attending a service. Studio attendants who carried her in her wheelchair up the winding staircases of Broadcasting House were always helpless with laughter at her stories.

Occasionally, I met contributors who thought my attempts at production and editing undermined their authority. Betty Cohen was the wife of a notable Cardiff solicitor; she had begun writing short talks on her twin interests: growing orchids and tatting. Immaculately groomed in a structured sort of way, not a wisp of blonde hair out of place, she was elegant, charming and gracious, albeit slightly intimidating. When I had the temerity to suggest small changes to strengthen her script, her countenance hardened, her lips formed a pencil-thin line, and her steely gaze became fixed somewhere between the bridge of my nose and my left ear lobe.

'What do you know about writing?' she asked crisply. I was about to reply when the lips moved again. 'What did you do before coming to the BBC?'

'Agricultural Botany.'

'Huh,' she puffed, 'I knew there was something odd about you.'

We made our peace. It was all part of the give and take, the developing trust between producer and contributor, and, overall, I learned a good deal from the people I met and those I worked with.

There was little flexibility in the technological resources we had at our disposal to make speech programmes. We were studio-bound. Talks and interviews were tightly structured, written, prepared and well rehearsed before live transmissions, or, if necessary, were recorded on disc beforehand, but within two years of my becoming a producer, programme-making became easier and much more relaxed. The tape era had arrived. Machines could record for longer periods and we could edit the material. Using an ordinary razor-blade to cut the tape, we could remove fluffs, stumbles and words, change sentences around, and even lengthen speech pauses and intakes of breath, to make them sound more dramatic. Formality went out of the window.

Within months came portable tape recorders powered by batteries. These machines were housed in dark green cases weighing about twelve pounds, and according to the engineers who had developed the concept, could be carried easily by hanging them on a wide shoulder-strap. Many of us developed dropped shoulders from the effort of carrying them. They were called Midgets; no doubt, this was another acronym for a technical term. They came with detailed instructions for users, mainly reporters and producers, who were not trained technical people. Top of the list, typed in large red letters, was the statement, 'Sturdy, portable and reliable. Treat with care. This machine is robust but do not drop.'

Producers were liberated. We could interview people in their own environment, relaxed and at ease. A reel of tape could record twelve minutes of material, and tapes could be used repeatedly. Of course, there were flaws in this new technology, and more than once I was caught out by a battery running down without warning, making a precious recording sound like the strangulated howling of a Yeti. Worse, if the small, vicious handle on the lid's case misbehaved, a device that we could turn manually to rewind the reel was likely to stretch the tape until it resembled a ball of brown string.

Such a hiatus occurred during an interview with the prolific novelist, Bertha Ruck, a tall, raven-haired, imperious woman well into her eighties. She had just finished her morning swim in the waters of Cardigan Bay and was seated, back to the light, 'so that I can see you,' and was in mid-flow, recalling, with presenter Gwenyth Petty, her views on the Bloomsbury set, when I saw the reel of tape come to an end. She looked down at me, on the floor with my Midget, red-faced and flustered, laboriously trying to rewind.

'What are you doing down there, gel?' she boomed.

'She's got hay fever,' said Gwenyth helpfully, seeing my face getting redder and redder.

From my position on the floor, it was impossible to match her withering look.

Three

The fifties decade was noted in the broadcasting industry for change and development, much of it technological. Colour television was a supreme advance, as was the advent of VHF, or FM frequencies, as they became known (frequency modulated short wave broadcasting). At a stroke, VHF eliminated interference on radio airwaves, and it provided a capability for many more frequencies. Within a short time, a chain of transmitters offered trouble-free broadcasting to over ninety per cent of the population of Wales. However, despite the effort of Controller Wales to sell the new concept of VHF to listeners, which he proclaimed to predict a 'Very Happy Future', sales of new radio sets, which cost twice as much as ordinary sets, were extremely slow and remained so for many years.

Despite technological advances, the future for broadcasters remained problematic and uncertain. During a debate at Westminster, the Conservative MP Sir David Llewellyn used the occasion to bring the charge of bias in favour of Welsh Nationalism in news programmes. Broadcasting House was turned upside down while news editor Tom Richards and three colleagues amassed evidence to show there was no justification for the accusation. When they surfaced from that exercise, they were asked to find further evidence for the Pilkington Committee, a body established by the

Government to determine an operational structure for UK television, now that commercial television had come into existence. It was also an opportunity to consider the means of providing regional television.

The core issue facing the BBC in Wales, in the second half of the fifties decade, was how to provide an effective public service in two languages, on radio and television, and to compete vigorously against commercial television. The immediate problem was the need for new frequencies. Wales was attempting to justify a regular television service it could call its own. Welsh-language programmes, seven programmes a month at that time, were shown before the network opened at 7 o'clock in the evening, or, after the network close down at 11 p.m., as a kind of addendum to the BBC Television Service. On the other hand, commercial television had been organised as a network of regional companies. Granada, for instance, transmitted its television programmes to the north of England, but they had the added advantage, in terms of advertising revenue, of extended coverage in north Wales. In 1958, TWW, Television Wales and the West, was the first company to win the franchise to provide television programmes for Wales and the West Country. It was a matter of genuine concern to BBC Wales's executives, who believed the new commercial television company would soon be seen as a more effective provider of a service for Wales.

The political activity increased in intensity. Broadcasting issues in Wales were complex because of the Welsh language and the need to increase the number and widen the range of programmes. From the time of the very first radio broadcast in February 1923, from a studio in Cardiff, to the establishment of Wales as a region in 1937, the relationship with Head Office in London had been uneasy. Much of the agitation and pressure to improve the broadcasting service in Wales came from Welsh speakers, but Sir John Reith, the architect and creator of public service broadcasting, was a centralist, and when he eventually agreed that a radio wavelength should be allocated to Wales, he commented that his decision had been based on the 'everlasting Welsh trouble'. Many leading producers of that time in London held similar views, believing that only programmes produced in London were worth hearing. The campaigns of those years, led by politicians and leading academics, ensured that the landmark decision to establish a separate wavelength for Wales within the public service broadcasting system would enhance the national identity. It may have been a true and worthwhile victory, but the Reithian concept of a centralised organisation remained the governance for those who had to administer its affairs. Autonomy was restricted. In the nineteen-forties, Head Office controlled all capital expenditure. Salary scales for regional producers were lower than for London producers, and although there were calls for greater freedom, the centre's grip on finance, accommodation and staff remained firm. After the war, calls for greater freedom and devolution to control our own broadcasting affairs were a recurring theme.

When, in 1958, Controller Wales saw the competition for audiences from the new commercial station, TWW, he used it as another opportunity to influence the BBC's hierarchy in London to allocate more resources for Wales. Alun Davies was a man of stature and experience. A tall man, six feet five inches, missing by one inch the title of being the tallest staff man in the BBC, he had already accumulated ten years' experience as Controller (the head of establishment) in 1955. For the first time in his experience, the battles of the fifties and the early part of the sixties were to occupy most of his energies until his retirement. His tallness and the seriousness of his countenance gave him a quality of unbending remoteness; he was able to distance himself from ordinary mortals, but he was the right man at the right time to carry the broadcasting banner for Wales. He was a man of probity, the son of a Congregational minister, dependable and of high moral principles. He could argue his case with fairness, cogency and resolute tenacity but, in more relaxed company, he was warm, with a gentle sense of humour, always concerned for the well-being of his staff. His management team, which constitutionally did not change much for the next twenty-five years, included the post of Head of Programmes, the holder of which was responsible for radio and television output in Welsh and English. There was an Assistant Head of Programmes, a Head of Engineering, and a post called the Welsh Executive, a term for what is today the Head of Corporate Affairs.

Ernest Jenkins, the Welsh Executive, had been a BBC staff member for thirty years. Once upon a time, he had been Uncle Ernie to his young fans listening to *Children's Hour*, but with approaching retirement, he had turned himself into the archetypal administrator. White-haired, he had a round, shiny face, indeed, a round body that was always clothed in a navy three-piece-suit. He sat from 9.00 in the morning behind his brightly polished desk, which was empty of office paraphernalia and paper until the morning break for coffee at 10.45. That first period of the day was acknowledged as his *Daily Mirror* time. During my first week, he gave me a document of staff rules and instructions and, as I left his office, he said, 'When you've read those, don't lose your innocence.'

I puzzled over that one, but Heber, as he was known, I think it was his middle name, had an inborn skill for making pithy comments. During a staff meeting chaired by the Controller, he summed up a discussion on the future of radio, and the need for additional frequencies in Wales, with a sly dig at the elitist and expensive new network, the Third Programme.

'Controller, the Third Programme can be heard in Cyncoed Road, Cardiff, with alarming clarity.'

Heber's retirement gave the Controller an opportunity to exercise his ruthless hand by announcing, to a surprised staff meeting, a new management team. Watkin Jones, who had been Head of Programmes for ten years, was to become the Welsh Executive, and Hywel Davies, Lorraine's husband and the present Assistant Head, was to take over responsibility for all programme output. The meeting held its corporate breath. It was sudden and unexpected. There had been no advertisement for the top job, no interviews, not a hint of playing the fair-play game. By today's standards, it was decisive and yet benign. The majority agreed it was high time for a change, and everyone respected and admired Hywel Davies. He chose as his Assistant Head of Programmes an experienced and creative talks producer based in Swansea, writer and poet Aneirin Talfan Davies.

Then came the fall-out. Lorraine, married to Hywel, found her position as *Children's Hour* Organiser untenable. The BBC's administrative structure, based on principles developed by the civil service, had an arcane system of rules and regulations designed to sustain and organise a community of programme makers. The bureaucratic machine in London managed to put rules in place to fit any situation. Marriage was one. A couple, who were both members of staff on the same salary grade, could work together, but if one became a manager with authority over the other, leaving the organisation was the only option. Lorraine took the cue and, as a result, broadcasting in Wales lost its most creative and challenging radio producer. Earlier in her career, she had been the victim of another rule. Cardiff had wished to appoint her as Drama Producer, but London refused to ratify their decision. She could remain in her present post, they said, but because her husband was a member of BBC staff, she was not allowed to move to a new one.

Local conditions and rules were designed to preserve the power structure and to ease the bureaucratic operation. At lunchtime, Broadcasting House resembled a great liner of pleasure with two sittings for lunch. It was called the 'divide and eat policy'. The canteen was small, adapted from the front room of one of the three houses. Two sittings reflected a notable pecking order. Secretaries, studio attendants and engineers – those on lower salary grades – ate at 12.30, and producers, administrators and senior staff ate at 1.15. Lunchtime procedures were a matter of necessity but, occasionally, one felt rules were the result of whims. For instance, women were forbidden to wear trousers, even during the windiest outside broadcasts. One or two grand ladies, such as Mai Jones, wore hats to meetings and to direct in studio, and any secretary arriving late for work in the morning immediately felt the lash of Mag Watkins's tongue. She was a rather austere, straight-talking lady from Cardiganshire, who took her responsibilities very seriously, making sure the secretarial support system was functioning correctly. At five to nine, she would place herself in the bay window of the office above the canteen, light her Craven A cigarette, and any late arrival was noted, telephoned and asked to account for herself. A persistent culprit like Kitty Hughes, a seasoned 'night before' lady, was able to weave wonderfully imaginative stories about her exploits on the No. 23 bus, which even cunning Mag Watkins failed to punish.

Hywel Davies took up his appointment as Head of Programmes almost immediately, bringing a fresh impetus and vision to programming. He was ultimately responsible for the work of producers and their programmes on radio and television, in both languages. He was undeterred by a lack of finance for his plans, and he sought opportunities to maximise effort from meagre resources in order to increase the number of programme productions. He decreed that radio producers, especially those in key departments such as sport, children and religion, should also produce television programmes. We would become what he called ambidextrous; our contribution would add to the output of six fully trained television producers. It was a key decision, and for me, an excellent opportunity to learn the techniques of being a television producer/director and presenter.

Following Lorraine's departure, a new Head of Children's programmes was appointed, with Evelyn Williams remaining as deputy. Ifan O. Williams was a gifted all-rounder in radio and television, a people person, a populist with a wonderful reputation as an interviewer and presenter of programmes. He also possessed a short fuse and an ingrained impatience in his dealings with rules and regulations, especially those devised by cautious engineers and autocratic administrators. 'Flying by the seat of his pants,' was an apt description of Ifan directing in the gallery. For that reason, and that reason alone, he was not a gifted teacher, but he was fun, creative and he flirted outrageously. He and Evelyn were invited to produce a Welsh-language, weekly, half-hour children's programme for transmission at lunchtime on Saturdays, a period before the main network television channel opened. They coined the umbrella title, *Telewele*, a new word for the Welsh lexicon, helped by members of a committee set up to devise suitable names and translations for new technical words. The same committee, a few years earlier, had established the word *teledu* for television.

Evelyn and I were introduced into the mysteries of television, in Studio B gallery, when Ifan held forth on camera angles, vision mixing, lighting and sound. His usual lucidity deserted him when he saw incomprehension settle on our faces, and his impatience surfaced. Television was easy. It was simply a matter of putting pictures on words. Evelyn was immensely experienced as a radio producer and writer. She abhorred slovenly language, she was meticulous and a perfectionist, and this haphazard lesson went against all her principles. However, before she could take issue, Ifan decided that I was to direct the live edition of *Telewele* the following day. He handed me the script. Controlling my panic, I turned the pages one by one. The first page contained sparse instructions for three opening title captions, and the last page had similar instructions for closing titles. In between there were twelve almost blank ones. The heart of the camera script contained the words: 'As directed' (supposedly by me), opposite 'Ifan interviews Mary Jones about fly-fishing.'

'You can't go wrong,' he said impatiently. 'You'll watch me.'

It would have been impossible not to. He was presenting the programme.

The following morning, after a sleepless night counting camera shots, I sat biting my nails in the gallery high above the studio, looking at two blank screens, knowing two cameramen in the studio below were waiting for instructions. Evelyn, who had come to observe and to offer support, sat white-faced, straight-backed and beautifully groomed, knowing she would be next – next week. I heard the engineer, John Jones, mutter under his breath on the talk back to his technical crew.

'We've drawn the very short straw this time, boys. Do your best.'

Thanks to the 'boys', we muddled through, mixing wide angles, mid-shots and close-ups, not in fast succession, or well framed, not even well lit, but enough of them to fill twenty-five minutes. These full-of-faults live programmes were among the first regular, weekly, general-interest programmes to be transmitted from the BBC's developing studio complex, a converted chapel about a mile from Broadcasting House, in an area of the city called Broadway. The rows of small terraced houses around the chapel were in sharp contrast to the American dream factory. Studio A, where congregations had once listened to fiery sermons, was a large studio used for drama and light entertainment, where talented directors pushed its capabilities to the limit during live transmissions. Studio B, once the vestry, was smaller, considered suitable for magazine programmes of all types. It was where Ifan, Evelyn and I, in turn, produced a variety of programmes on very small budgets, from intricate puppet shows to nature and scientific programmes, sport and magic.

There were opportunities aplenty in this ambidextrous world, and I revelled in it all. I began spreading my wings into other areas of programming. Somehow or other, I managed to concoct a weekly fifteen minute television programme for women, *Gwraig y Tŷ*, with staff announcer Nest Owen as presenter. Moreover, I was soon involved with the farming radio and television output for Wales and the network. It was the happiest of times, when I was out, getting to know the highways and byways of Wales, meeting people and understanding the huge changes taking place in the agricultural industry. The high point was the Royal Welsh Agricultural Show, held in July, in those years, at a different location every year. By coincidence, my first experience of the problems involved in covering the three-day event on radio was at Aberystwyth, my home territory, at an idyllic site on the wide, flat acres of estuary land around the river Rheidol. The BBC had erected a small stand and studio. I was to assist Alun Davies, an experienced sports producer and reporter, with an interest in matters of the countryside. The first sunny day went well, but overnight, sustained downpours created havoc. Water cascaded from the surrounding hills to meet a particularly high tide; the river overflowed its banks and turned the site, in a matter of hours, into a gigantic lake. They called for boats from the harbour, and stock judging in water was suspended.

Until the floods subsided, Alun and his journalist presenter, J. C. Griffith Jones, decided to while away the time in the nearest hospitality tent. Morning turned into late afternoon. Transmission time approached and the sound engineer turned to me. 'You'd better take over,' he said.

Because I had gained a degree of confidence, I replied nonchalantly, 'They'll be back, and, anyway, we have no material to transmit.'

The engineer was well used to dealing with little upstarts like me, the public service ethos was deeply ingrained, and he scolded.

'It is our duty. We have to do it.'

At four-thirty, they staggered back. Alun's Wellingtons, on the wrong feet, were at odds with his body, and J. C. Griffith Jones, his sombre, black Anthony Eden hat at a jaunty angle, was caked in mud. They held each other upright, slowly making their way to the office space, and together they fell, poleaxed, into a deep sleep, to snore, oblivious to the mounting panic around them. Somehow or other, we got a programme together by 7.15 p.m. As I introduced a report by Harry Soan, I heard a slurred shout from deep darkness beyond the studio echo across the airwaves, 'Th… em, Tha… em, Tha… em, Tha wa… was Test… Yes… Yesterday.'

A deafening crash followed. Alun had pulled the typewriter on his head.

The reorganisation and fresh impetus generated by Hywel Davies brought to the screen a regular television, weekday news programme, and I became a participant as a reporter, mainly on farming topics, and issues that were more light-hearted. I entered the world of journalism. The programme, called *Beunydd* (Daily), was produced by the journalist, poet and author, T. Glynne Davies, from the chapel's broom cupboard under the stairs. The one camera, which had seen better days in London, probably at the Coronation, was a gigantic Cyclops with three lenses that dominated the small, claustrophobic sauna of a studio. The first bulletin transmitted from there was the English news programme presented by Michael Aspel, produced by Wynford Jones and John Ormond, and it was deemed a major step forward for television in Wales.

The benign spirit of the chapel's past must have protected us from thinking too deeply about our crazy approach to the production of a daily, Welsh-language, news programme. There were many close calls. The studio was at least a mile away from the newsroom in Broadcasting House, and this was where stories for the bulletin, typed on yellow A4 pages, were prepared. Transmission was at 1 o'clock. A taxi on stand-by outside the front door began revving up from 12.15, but T. Glynne operated the good journalist maxim that news should be last minute and up to date. The fast taxi journey, more often than not, a few minutes after 12.30, was always regarded as the first rehearsal, as Glynne tried to shuffle his sheaf of paper into a cohesive running order with one hand, while holding a cigarette with the other. The studio was ready and lined up, with a crew bracing themselves for their daily dose of bedlam, as we reporters and newsreader attempted to decide how to seat each other in the cramped space. The Cyclops had one basic movement, a pan to the right and a pan to the left, so that seating became a neat jigsaw, a lottery, or both, depending on whether T. Glynne changed the running order at the very last minute. When we saw his masterly organisational powers with the studio chairs, we soon realised that reporter Alan Protheroe was destined for greatness; he went on to an illustrious career in the London news operation and later as Deputy Director General.

Contributors sat in line, with the newsreader at one end. Occasionally, a chair for a live interview was added. When transmission of the fifteen-minute programme began, no-one could move. The newsreader would read the bulletin's first news stories before introducing Alan for his report. The camera panned left to his chair. So far, so good. When Alan talked to his interviewee, the camera panned left again. When time was up, the camera panned right, returning its lens to focus on the newsreader. The interesting bit for camera and contributors was when my turn came, at the far end of the line. The Cyclops would pan slowly, passing Alan, also the interviewee, usually caught slumped in his chair from the trauma of it all, before finally reaching me. The returning pan movement, after I completed my piece, would reveal stark faces, hungry for lunch.

Contact between studio and gallery, or newsreader and producer, was by an old army telephone, which had to be manually wound on air to make it ring. Film was often played in from machines in Bristol or London, and hiatus would be heaped on hiatus, if operators in these centres failed to pick up the correct Welsh-language cue to start running the film. One producer, working on another programme, devised a fail-safe procedure. He ordered his presenter to produce a white handkerchief from his pocket as a sign to, 'Run Telecine'. It was ambidexterity carried to extreme limits. We knew little about television technology but there was energetic commitment in abundance coupled with a fierce camaraderie.

One edition of the children's *Telewele* series I produced in these tempestuous times has earned an honoured place in the archives of BBC Wales. It was 1958, a day or so before November 5th, and our aim was to give an insight into the historical background of Guy Fawkes's act of treason, and to explain how fireworks, in their myriad forms, were made. The emphasis was on safety. Two leading Welsh scientists, seasoned television contributors Dr Glyn O. Phillips and Gwilym Humphreys, were engaged to present and to carry out simple experiments in the studio. The rehearsal went well. The small amount of carbon and iron filings placed in a paper cone ignited and reacted as expected. I was quietly confident, reassured by the ease with which my camera directions followed the action. Everything augured well.

The programme was being recorded to a videotape machine called Ampex, which was located in Lime Grove in London. Cardiff did not possess this facility. Distance, however, was not a problem, and would only become one should we have an unexpected incident during the recording. In such a situation, the standard practice was to go back to the top of the programme and start again. What one did not do was edit the video tape, which meant physically cutting it, thereby making it useless for any further recording. To slice a tape was a heinous professional failure and a budgetary disaster. That seemingly simple act would cost £60. Considering that my programme budget was £65, it was obvious that the gap between professional acclaim and opprobrium was narrow. That programme was a 'one chance or else situation'. I was determined not to transgress the eleventh commandment, 'Thou shalt not cut the tape'.

Under such pressure, the adrenalin ran high, and the opening sequences could not have been more promising. The cameras worked, the sound was clear, the presenters were word-perfect, in those days when neither autocue nor teleprompt were available.

Glyn began his first demonstration. He filled the cone carefully with the mixture of carbon and iron filings and Gwilym handed him a lit taper. I punched up Camera One, and on screen the sparks danced and glowed to perfection. I cut to Camera Two for a wide angle of the scene, and, on the instant, a huge spark rose like a meteor from the depth of the cone and landed on a neat pile of fireworks at the other end of the table.

A Jacky Jumper spluttered into life, then a couple of bangers joined in, followed by a large, smoky sparkler. My wide angle on Camera Two wobbled as Mike, its operator, beat a fast retreat, to find refuge behind Harry on Camera One. Harry, however, had no desire to be in the front line, or to further his career with heroic gestures. On my monitor, I saw him discard his headphones and make a dash for safety, leaving his camera forlorn and abandoned. Then, Bill, the fireman, with a bucket of sand in one hand and a fire-extinguisher in the other, sped into shot. In stunned silence, we watched the mayhem beneath us. Camera One was swinging aimlessly, but Camera Two was holding steady focus on the pyrotechnics. The presenters were barely visible, engulfed in smoke. Three big rockets at the very end of the table were waiting to join the party.

'This is it,' I thought, 'the Big Bang. Studio B on the verge of a journey to the stars, but fireman Bill, with his sand and spray, postponed the apocalypse. As I sat there like a rabbit stunned, I heard John Jones, the technical manager, yell at me above the hissing and the bangs.

'Carry on! For God's sake, CARRY ON!'

'Where's Harry?' I yelled back at him.

'Bugger Harry. You've got Mike on Camera One, the smoke's

clearing. Carry on. You can't cut the bloody tape. REMEMBER?'

Glyn and Gwilym emerged from the gloom, blackened but unbowed. They carried on without deviating from the original plan and we ended the recording 'on time'.

The incident had taken one minute and twenty seconds, an aeon in production terms. There was no possibility of it being transmitted in its entirety, without adding explanatory commentary; an option not available to me. Neither was the option of editing the tape – dire as the consequences of that decision would be. The tape was in London. How was I to excise the studio calamity? How could I fill the unforgiving minute and twenty seconds? I decided that I would transmit up to the point where Gwilym passed the lighted taper to Glyn, then cutaway to some library film of a firework extravaganza. The strategy worked; that is what the audience in Wales saw on transmission. The crisis had passed, the tape remained uncut and I had got away with it – by a stroke of luck.

Mistakes in this business cannot be kept secret; they are public mistakes. Video recording engineers deep in the bowels of Lime Grove, London, could not believe the scene they saw enacted on screen in Cardiff. Knowledge of Welsh was not required. It was pure silent movie, Chaplinesque material.

They carried the tin of tape, like a precious jewel, to the production office of the nightly current affairs programme, *Tonight*. Producers and editors of that programme could not believe their luck at finding a scene of such misfortune and farce. They decided to show it, as a perfect and timely warning on safety, on November 5th. Without telling us, they presented it as an incident made by our 'colleagues in Wales'. As a result, we made the network, and we made it repeatedly.

Scientists Glyn and Gwilym were mortified. They felt they had been made to look incompetent fools and their professional status undermined. At first, they demanded an apology, and the tit-for-tat debate continued for days. The high-handed journalists in London had not sought permission, and the academics insisted on an embargo on further transmissions. For decades, the piece of tape was not allowed out of its tin without first reference to me, but copies had been made and passed from office to office. It has been shown regularly since. In fact, whenever vintage screen disasters are shown, and a certain elephant is seen rampaging around the hapless presenters in the *Blue Peter* studio, the fireworks in Wales disaster is not far behind.

Despite all the mishaps, I had proved I could work as a member of a team and, at the end of the fifties, I felt secure, fulfilled, with a job for life. I was a member of the established staff, and I had become more resilient and less reserved. I had learned to give and take. The work ethic had been ingrained from an early age; my father was a disciplined taskmaster who applauded personal motivation and made it a virtue not to be idle. Lorraine Davies had underlined the principle. If you didn't work, you didn't get and, as the years passed and I matured, I became frustrated at the lack of 'will and motivation' in others. It was through programme-making that I found a means of self-expression and individuality, although, on reflection, I allowed myself to do too much. I threw myself into every aspect of my work without allowing myself time to think and consider. I was pell-mell into the next programme, preparing to meet another deadline, almost before the radio waves of my last effort had settled into the ether.

My superiors obstructed any effort I made to change direction and to get more experience by moving to other production departments. I was not ambitious, but one or two opportunities came my way. The *Woman's Hour* editor offered me a three-month attachment to work in the London department, but Cardiff management refused to allow me to go. Later, T. Glynne Davies encouraged me to apply for the post of television director, to work with him in the news department. I was short-listed and given an interview but, a week or so later, I received a stark note of rejection. It was a blow and a huge disappointment. Surprisingly, within a few days, I received a summons to see the Controller, and I went up the golden staircase to his office on the third floor, a place of managerial quietness and sobriety.

That day, at my second-ever formal meeting with him on a one-to-one basis, he rose to his full height to greet me, and then proceeded to exercise the iron fist in the velvet glove technique: praise first, ask about your family second, and third, announce bad news and give excuses. I was told that I was by far the best candidate but, because of the needs of the service, the Board felt it right to keep me on the radio establishment and in my present post. He handed me a memo as a record of the decision, which he said would be placed in my personal file. To this day, I am not sure why I did not obtain the post. I comforted myself with the thought that the establishment was not ready to accommodate a woman in the rough and tumble of the news operation; nevertheless, the decision rankled for months. The man they appointed, with no experience of television, proved unsuitable and he left within a short time. I had missed a marvellous opportunity to enter television but there was plenty of compensation. I had fallen in love, and other opportunities were beckoning.

The Sixties

One

I met my husband David eighteen months before we welcomed the new decade. He had given up a history-teaching job to join the BBC as an announcer and newsreader. We were attracted, fell in love, and we married on St. David's Day. Within eighteen months, I was pregnant. When we became engaged, Hywel Davies, who had an eye for marketing an 'in house' romance, directed us to present a live, weekly record request programme together. To start work at half past eight on Tuesday mornings was enough to tax any developing relationship, but the audience liked the partnership, and the series, presented bilingually, continued for two years. I changed my name from Phillips to Bevan somewhere in the middle of the series. David was a Rhondda Valley man, who came from a line of teachers on his mother's side; his father was an administrator at the local hospital. He was an only child, whereas I was a rebellious middle sister, from a rural background steeped in countryside traditions. We thought differences in our backgrounds were strengths but, within a few years, differences in temperament and attitude caused strains and irritations.

Pregnancy changed every perspective, and as I look back today, I have no regrets that I decided to give up work to look after the baby. When I left the BBC in September 1961, it was impossible to predict whether I would ever return. I heard the words, 'The BBC doesn't owe you a living, and there are no guarantees in this business,' as I made the most of my last months as a working woman. I was three months pregnant when I agreed to present a series of television programmes from the Royal Welsh Agricultural Show. Producer Selwyn Roderick looked me up and down as though I was likely to present myself as an exhibit.

'You look normal,' he said, when he issued the invitation in May. As an afterthought, Selwyn, sometimes less than tactful, added, 'If your bump shows, we'll put you behind a bale of straw and shoot you there.'

These were times when pregnant mothers did not flaunt their condition. Clothes designed to hide all signs of growth, were large, unflattering, voluminous, free-flowing, dark coloured gowns that hung unfashionably from the shoulders. They clung to the body during the hot sticky days of summer and ballooned in the winds of winter. When the show opened in late July, my pregnancy was more than obvious. I conformed to protocol and I wore a dark navy 'maternity gown' glossed with a fake white rose on the yoke, giving the impression that I had won an award for best of breed. Selwyn looked at my dress and my condition, and ordered a wall of straw bales to be built. I stood behind it to make my opening introduction.

His last words to me before we went on air were prophetic.

'Look nonchalant,' he said, 'but be convincing,' and for three days, I had no idea whether I complied with the order. Behind the straw bales, I looked as though I was taking part in a fairground game, a bobbing-head target for coconuts.

I had mixed emotions in September, when I walked out of Broadcasting House for the last time. I was giving myself three months rest before the baby was due, in the first week of January.

I was committed to work, and I was equally committed to motherhood and family life, but it was almost impossible to combine both without a fail-safe support system. It was unfair to ask my mother-in-law, who lived close by, to take on the responsibility of full-time child minding. Prospective parents of those years were much influenced by the research of psychiatrist, John Bowlby, who produced evidence to indicate that the prolonged separation of a child from the mother during the first five years could lead to delinquency in later life. That kind of pronouncement, backed up by research, helped to foster immense guilt in women like me. In fact, a whole generation of mothers felt anguished as they contemplated making the choice between careers and motherhood. I was not ambitious. Women did not confess to such motives. Ambition was thought to be unfeminine, but I did hope that one day I would return to resume that particular and important part of my life. It was notable that although attitudes were slowly changing, it was the 'steady as you go', mainly childless types who 'got on'.

My pregnancy was normal, and I followed instructions from the antenatal classes to the letter, but at the clinic, I became involved in a medical experiment designed to evaluate the effect of hypnosis and deep relaxation on childbirth. Mr Evans, my consultant, believed the new techniques he was developing could benefit mother and baby, but he needed the co-operation of 'mothers to be', to provide evidence. I was sitting in the waiting area at the clinic one Tuesday morning when I heard a voice announce,

'Mr Evans would like volunteers for a special project he's conducting.' I bowed my head and moved in my seat, to hide behind a large back. The voice continued, 'Look, it won't take more than five minutes. He just wants to talk to you. Come on.'

There was a hint of exasperation in her voice.

No-one moved a muscle, and I heard my name.

'Mrs Bevan, you'll come, won't you? And you, Susan Crabb?'

I had been caught again. My surname had become a curse. The letter B, inevitably at the top of all lists, was the first to be called. I comforted myself with the thought that this time, a Bevan, no relation, was the architect of the Health Service. Susan Crabb, on the other hand, had no such high-minded thoughts; she was obviously a sharp blonde cookie.

'Sorry, nurse,' she said, 'my husband's waiting for me. We're going shopping.' When I looked around, the clinic had suddenly emptied.

Sheepishly, I was led to the consultant's room, my dark navy dress looking as out of place as it had on the show ground. Mr Evans could only be described as dishy. Tall, distinguished-looking, he had a nice, open, kindly face, greying hair at the temples; he wore a pristine white coat with natural authority. He looked a little like film star Tyrone Power, and I melted as I listened to his words.

'Giving birth requires a high level of relaxation. My technique will help you and the baby. Our aim is to avoid stress.'

I believed him. He was so handsome.

I settled gingerly into a deep leather chair and he took me through a series of exercises. I looked at a spot on the ceiling, I breathed deeply, and I counted up to ten. 'NOW,' he said, 'you are deeply relaxed.'

I was surprised. How did he know? Then, the moment passed. Next, he encouraged me to lift my left arm to a position above my head. His voice was mesmerising, warm and gentle, and although I felt I could, at will, disobey his instructions for making me look so ridiculous, I didn't.

'You are a star,' he told me, at the end of the first session, and with that kind of commendation, I agreed to take part in his experiment. I followed his instructions for four months. I was so scared of the pain of childbirth that I was ready to try anything. At one session, he told me the skin on the back of my left hand would become numb. 'As proof,' I heard his voice say, 'I shall touch it with a sharp instrument.' I felt nothing. Then he touched my right hand and I recoiled. It was, of course, the same needle touching both hands. In time, I graduated from looking at spots on the ceiling in order to begin the relaxation process, to concentrating on my wedding ring, and I learnt to relax deeply without the help of his voice. As a reward, the cover of my clinical file carried a huge red star, a sign to everyone that I was 'the consultant's special'.

Within three weeks of the expected birth, Mr Evans asked one more favour of me. Would I help medical science by joining him at a lecture he was giving to a few of his colleagues? I said yes, reluctantly. By this time, I was heavy and large, not a pretty sight and, as I feared, it turned out to be an excruciating experience. The few had turned into two hundred. Formally seated in serried ranks in a lecture theatre, they had come from every hospital and midwifery department in South Wales. Mr Evans had discarded his white coat for a superbly cut, charcoal-grey suit, a pale blue shirt and a Welsh School of Medicine tie. He walked up and down distractedly, and was obviously in need of a dose of his own 'little exercises'. He told me to wait outside the lecture theatre until he had completed his introductory remarks.

'You don't want to listen to me. Relax,' he ordered, 'I'll call you when I'm ready.'

When that time came, I shuffled onto the stage and sank into an armchair. Two hundred pairs of eyes looked down at me, my dress ballooned. I was not wearing stockings, because I couldn't bear a suspender belt anywhere near the bulge, and my feet were unable to reach the floor. I closed my eyes and Mr Evans began. My eyelids twitched uncontrollably as I attempted to look a picture of relaxed repose, and I believe I finished the routine, raising my arms like windmills, in record time. No-one clapped and I galloped out, leaving the audience to consider their thoughts on medical progress and to wonder at Mr Evans's mystic gifts.

A month later, at the first hint of a labour pain, I went into Glossop Terrace Maternity Hospital, and the red star on my file brought Mr. Evans to my bedside at ten o'clock that night.

'Why not relax and have a sleep?' he said. 'Look at your wedding ring.'

I looked, breathed deeply, counted to ten and I was asleep before the next pain engulfed me. I slept until an hour before the birth. Mr Evans had left strict instructions to be called when I awoke, but he was dealing with an emergency in theatre at another hospital at the critical time. Instead, we spoke on the telephone, and at the sound of his voice, the pains that were gathering strength for the final push became bearable. It was unfortunate he was not present when Huw arrived, weighing 6 lbs. 6 ozs, at 05.30 on Friday, January 5th. In a cloud of relief, joy, and 'gas and air,' I felt I had done my little bit for medical progress.

Life changed for David and me. It was complete happiness; we were no longer a couple; we were a family. We lived in a three-bedroom, detached house on a modern housing estate called Pantmawr Garden Village. This was not a picturesque village location, it did not even have the makings of one, but it was a rather undistinguished suburban enclave, part of the sixties building boom on the foothill of Caerphilly Mountain, on the outskirts of Cardiff. The house was architecturally functional, but we longed for trees and gardens to mature, to disguise all those straight-lined frontages and fences, fertile ground for leylandii planting. It was a new community of youthful, married couples with young children, and it was easy to make friends. Many women, like me, had given up work for motherhood, the notion of feminism had been put on hold, and the American guru, Dr Benjamin Spock, wrote our Bible on parenthood and child rearing.

Mothers often met to share common experiences, usually once a fortnight at the baby clinic, a long mobile caravan that parked in the lay-by alongside the shops. Occasionally, they turned into nightmarish bedlam, especially when babies had their vaccination injections, and the caravan shook like a piece of flotsam in a tornado. It was small, crowded and hot. In winter, it steamed, in summer, it baked. An appointments system was a notion for the future, and we waited our turn, squashed together on narrow benches arranged around the sides of the van. Dressing a baby in comfort was impossible, and I envied long-legged women who created level laps like platforms, and whose babies gurgled with contentment as hands worked gently over them. My lap was an incline on the move, and attempting to place a towelling nappy on Huw, while gripping a vicious safety pin between my teeth, became a matter of survival rather than a labour of love.

The first nine months had a momentum all of their own, with

different emotions and responsibilities. It was the time when I was exclusively a mother and I concentrated on the essentials of life. Domesticity almost turned me into a Persil Mum as I washed nappies and bathed Huw every morning, and I wheeled my large Silver Cross pram with bleached pride around the estate in the afternoons. The joy of the first smile and the relief at the appearance of the first tooth were signs of a normal development. The maternal instinct, which I didn't think I possessed to any great degree before my pregnancy, surfaced strongly. I learnt tolerance and patience just by watching his progress, letting him do things in his own time, making those attempts towards understanding and independence. It was a feeling of security, continuity and of belonging. I was directly shaping and influencing another life.

We spoke Welsh to Huw. We both came from Welsh-speaking families; communicating in the language, its history, culture and literature formed an inherent part of our lives. We were also aware that there had been a rapid decline in the number of Welsh speakers in the twentieth century, more especially in the ever-expanding urban areas. Our household was a Welsh-speaking island in Pantmawr Garden Village. I recollect less than half a dozen other families who spoke the language naturally, every day. In the opinion of many of our neighbours, education through the medium of Welsh was a waste of resources and finance, when the majority could speak English. These were becoming well-rehearsed arguments in a rapidly changing society. As far as we were concerned, the inheritance of a language and culture was precious. The first Welsh school in Cardiff had been established some years previously, and it had been agreed that a second would be opened in a neighbouring estate when Huw reached the age of four.

The distinguished nationalist writer and academic, Saunders Lewis, made by far the most dramatic pronouncement on the state of the Welsh language and its decline, in 1962, when the BBC invited him to deliver the Annual Radio Lecture. It had a seismic effect. Speaking slowly, in a thin, arresting voice, he declared that the future and the status of the language could only be secured by using revolutionary methods and direct action. Saunders Lewis was well-versed in such tactics. He had been charged and sentenced to nine months' imprisonment at the Old Bailey, in 1936, for attempting to burn down the Penyberth Bombing School in Lleyn, north Wales. The impact of his lecture was decisive. I listened to the radio that night in February, with Huw at my side, a mere six weeks old. It focused my mind and crystallised my thoughts. The meaning of nationhood was paramount, as was the importance of continuity and heritage. In a sense, I grew up. I was also free to express my views openly, not confined any longer by the regulatory powers of a large broadcasting organisation where expressing political views was forbidden. Later in the year, Cymdeithas yr Iaith Gymraeg (the Welsh Language Society) was born, and, almost immediately, began a campaign of law-breaking activities. Although by nature I tend to conform, the 'cause' stirred rebellious emotions within me. The language had become a priority issue. I became a sympathiser, but not, I fear, a front line participator.

Nevertheless, 1962 was not finished yet. It provided one other seismic event. As the year ended, panic gripped the world. President Kennedy and President Kruschev were resorting to political brinkmanship over the issue of Russia's intention to establish a nuclear-missile base in Cuba. Ships, with their deadly cargo on board, could be seen sailing towards the Caribbean island. The discord of the cold war was warming up, minute by minute, into the possibility of horrifying, worldwide carnage and decimation. It was happening before our eyes, invading our homes on television screens, and, within days, the world seemed to be on the brink of Armageddon. I had never experienced such fear.

Two

In two years, I became restless. The chores of motherhood may have become less demanding, but maternal exhaustion and irritation seemed to be taking over. Two-year-old toddlers are independent little beings; they may be mobile, but they have little good sense. The endless wrestling match to put on their clothes, to stop them drawing on the bedroom wall and persuade them to eat greens at lunch was sapping the energy; but engaging with an innocent mind, enthralled with the process of discovering more about the world, was more than compensation. Returning to full-time work was not an option at that stage, and I lacked the confidence and the cheek to tout my skills around the broadcasting fraternity, asking for *ad hoc* work as a producer or presenter. In my spare time, I turned to writing. I had always been interested in the entertainment scene, and I had viewed a new comedy/satirical television series produced by Jack Williams with curiosity. *Stiwdio B* included short sketches, monologues, topical and satirical songs; and whenever I gleaned time from potty training and building Lego castles, I set about doodling and writing sketches. Most of them went into the waste paper basket, but a few I sent to producer Jack Williams. I got used to my work being rejected but, at last, two sketches were accepted. The thrill of seeing words of mine, spoken by characters I'd created, come to life on screen was an emotion I had never truly experienced. It was pure joy. Jack was a thorough editor and producer, but just as I was coming to grips with the discipline of writing, an unexpected offer came my way.

Dorothy Williams, one of my closest friends, who was senior producer with the commercial television company TWW, telephoned to ask a special favour. At very short notice, would I present two programmes she was producing that week? Dorothy had been a good friend from our years at university in Bangor. She had worked initially with the BBC in London as a Studio Manager, and then transferred to do the same work at Cardiff. We had shared the same room in a B and B in a house in Richmond Road, run by the James family. She survived Lorraine's demanding instructions for studio effects, such as opening doors and running up and down steps, to illuminate the action for hair-raising children's adventure plays. When the opportunity came, Dorothy left for television, joining TWW as one of the company's first recruits. 'Please,' she pleaded on the telephone. 'I'm desperate.'

The urgency concerned two Welsh-language, light-hearted, game-show programmes, part of a series. Two teams of four people, from two different towns, pitted their wits, and played games before an invited audience of partisan followers. Myfanwy Howell, the doyenne of presenters, had been struck by illness, and the two programmes were scheduled for recording in two days' time. I should have said 'No' in a loud voice, but a combination of Dorothy's persuasive powers and my ego took over. I had never once presented a light entertainment programme, and the next two days were fraught and daunting. It was a matter of how to generate slick timing, keeping the pace of the programme moving, and sticking to the correct studio presentation moves. There was so much to remember. I got through the day, but a week later, when I was wallowing in the relief of completing the programmes, Dorothy invited me to present the whole series, and this led to a three-year association with TWW as a freelance presenter. My mother-in-law agreed to look after Huw on my working days, and, like all doting grandmothers, she could handle him with ease. They forged a wonderful relationship.

The atmosphere at TWW's Pontcanna studios was liberating, and not so hierarchical or as engulfed with correctness as the BBC. A few of their executives and directors were steeped in the entertainment business; they believed in popular programmes; and the company, through its Welsh Board, had a strong commitment to the Welsh language. Their programmes won audiences with their skill and professionalism, and during my three years with the company, I learnt a few hard-nosed lessons about making light entertainment programmes. They were aggressively commercial; good ratings brought profit; and time was money. They made maximum use of their studio resources, and we would record a minimum of two, usually four, editions of a quiz or game show in an afternoon. I had never seen myself as a game-show host. I don't think I ever became one, either. Not the snazzy, sequined, shining, sexy, wide-eyed, full of bubble and hype type, I was not glamorous, and I was not tall and thin, but for one reason or another, the camera liked me. That's what directors told me at the time, and I believed them. The daytime, afternoon Welsh-language shows, transmitted around teatime, suited me. They were low key, comfortable and warm, but the cardinal rule, drummed into me before every recording, was to fix a wide smile on my face, not to stray from the 'moves' and to 'keep the thing moving'.

A lapse of concentration was cruelly punished. One of my most cringing moments occurred during a recording of a children's quiz. A winsome twelve-year-old boy needed only one more correct answer in order to hit the jackpot. The lights dimmed and the drums rolled to heighten the tension, and I asked the last question to a hushed studio, 'What is the name of Shakespeare's wife?'

Quick as a flash, the boy answered confidently, 'Anne Boleyn'.

'CORRECT!' I shouted, and the triumphal blast of music and drums turned into a long discordant wail, the studio stuck at half-light, and Camera One, pointing at me, shook violently. A sudden clatter behind the set brought Mr Alun Mathias, the most unassuming of academics, running, arms waving, to centre stage, his face contorted with anguish, unable to speak coherently. Alun devised the questions, and this ghastly mistake, now committed to tape, could ruin his reputation for care and correctness.

'STOP!' a voice boomed in the studio over the talkback. It was Dorothy. She ran from the directing gallery into the studio and took me aside. 'You've had a lapse of concentration,' she whispered kindly.

Our friendship survived. The incident was dealt with quickly and effectively, we redid the sequence, using a different set of questions, and the boy easily won his jackpot prize.

Television presentation in those days, without auto cues and the trappings of technical modernity, was not an exact craft. The unexpected happening during live programmes was a constant peril. Well-rehearsed routines often turned into disordered farragoes, calling for skilful inventiveness. I was involved with a long-running natural history series in which we dealt with environmental and rural topics. Rarely did we film on location. The use, on a regular basis, of specially shot illustrative material was too costly and too time-consuming for the small production unit. We coped by bringing examples of flora and fauna to the studio.

My co-presenter, farmer James Thomas from Carmarthenshire, was asked one day to bring a hedgehog to the studio. James could be relied upon to find needles in haystacks, and finding a domiciled hedgehog was one of the simpler missions. The following Tuesday, the morning of transmission, he opened a cardboard box in the studio, and, to his surprise, he discovered the hedgehog he had brought had given birth to three little ones during the journey from deepest Carmarthen. We whooped with joy at the possibilities for television this increase in the hedgehog population had given us.

Mother was fed, the babies were content, and when we went on air, the family was tucked up in a bed of straw in the cardboard box, now painted bright blue and fuchsia pink for gender correctness. Our introduction to the programme was accompanied by images of mother and babies sleeping soundly, and James launched into the first item on the management of woodland. Off screen, I studied my script, in readiness for the hedgehogs. Out of the corner of my eye, I caught sight of movement in the garish box. I leaned forward. To my horror, I saw the mother swallowing her babies one by one. Three gulps and they were gone. The cue to begin the hedgehog item came at that moment, and, with all the aplomb of a paid-up member of Cool Cymru, I told viewers the newly born babies were deeply asleep, 'as was their custom,' in deep straw. It was a moment of no return. James, his face contorted with surprise, felt the strength of my toe hit his leg as he was about to put his hand in the straw. He missed seeing the carnage in the box but took the cue and we got through the programme. I had witnessed a mother hedgehog's natural defence mechanism after giving birth. Facing extreme danger, she takes extreme action. This one must have interpreted the noise and the hot, bright lights of a television studio as her entrance into Hades.

1964, the year I began my freelance work with TWW, was the year when the BBC in Wales got its own television wavelength and David became a television producer. A new transmitter opened at Wenvoe, outside Cardiff, to transmit programmes 'made in Wales for Wales' to Wales's viewers. A new expansion programme was underway as the Wenvoe transmitter increased the possibility of producing more programmes in Welsh and English. Twenty new television posts were advertised and over eight hundred people applied. David was appointed one of four producers with a brief to establish a new English language current affairs series. Despite the excitement and the anticipation for the expanded BBC Wales television channel, the service did not solve the linguistic problem. Welsh-language programmes would be shown on an English channel, the BBC 1 of today. In a population of two and a half million people, only approximately three quarters of a million spoke Welsh. Transmissions of programmes in Welsh could only be achieved by opting out, or displacing, popular network programmes at peak times. Many viewers, the majority of whom did not speak Welsh, felt it an imposition to be made to sit through programmes in a language they didn't understand. Many viewers had no choice. BBC Wales television was their only channel. It heralded almost two decades of protest and tension from viewers who felt short-changed by the public service broadcasting licence fee. Others, living in South Wales, soon found solace by turning their television aerials towards the West Country and the Mendip transmitter, to enjoy uninterrupted viewing from the West Region and the Bristol studios. In many respects, it became a nightmare scenario for broadcasters, as they tried to please most of the people, most of the time.

Hywel Davies, the man at the helm, had pushed through his programme of reform and recruitment in order to meet the official opening deadline of 9 February 1964. In our household, the excitement was intense as preparations for the new topical series with David at the helm, which they titled *Week In, Week Out,* gathered momentum. The team was influenced, as were many topical programmes of the time, by the success of a programme format devised by the producer Ned Sherrin, *That Was the Week that Was*. A challenging series, with new writers, presented by new faces. Attitudes, conventions, events, people, especially establishment figures, were questioned and satirised unmercifully. A similar concept formed the basis for the Wales version, with new writers and performers. During the first run, one or two sacred cows received the treatment, enough to generate vociferous reaction and criticism from some sections of the audience. It was risk-taking, but Hywel Davies was by no means dismissive, he was encouraged, and at the end of the run, he ordered a second series.

Three

I had managed to achieve the right balance between work and motherhood, due to flexible freelance arrangements with TWW. I had been given the opportunity to taste a wide range of opportunities and experiences, when the liberating sixties were in full swing, and the old order and structures were changing for good. It was becoming a decade of fun and crazy idealism and we were beginning to enjoy freedom from stifling conformity. Family life seemed beleaguered, traditional values were being questioned, but somehow they survived. Huw was four years old, enjoying his first weeks at school, when another phone call from another good friend changed the direction of my life again, this time irrevocably. Marion Griffith Williams, today known as Marion Eames, the author of popular Welsh historical novels, was moving from her post as a general programmes producer to be responsible for radio features. It caused a short-term vacancy, and a replacement was a matter of urgency. They needed an experienced producer for a weekly series of programmes, *Merched yn Bennaf* (Mainly for Women). Was I able to oblige until a permanent replacement could be appointed?

The request was a huge boost to my morale, but there were many practical problems to overcome. It was not the time to disturb Huw's routine at school, nor to rely on others to look after him at the end of the day. Before I accepted the commitment, I asked not to be held to the 9 to 5 office working hours. An enlightened management, or a desperate one, confirmed that I could be as flexible as was necessary, but transmissions and programme standards were paramount. TWW understood my reason for leaving. I did not have a binding contract with them, and at the time, I was not involved with another series. I took the BBC offer. Within ten days, I had a splendid office and a secretary in the newly opened Broadcasting House in Llandaff. In 1967, I felt like a new girl, beginning a new job, all over again.

There had been dramatic changes since I had left the BBC five years previously. Hywel Davies, who had so dominated the activities of BBC Wales with his vision, verve and insight, died tragically in 1965 at the age of forty-six. Lorraine, his widow, had returned to work, to become the radio drama producer. Ironically, this was the post she had been refused a decade earlier, due to BBC correctness. Aneirin Talfan Davies had taken over as Head of Programmes. Alun Oldfield Davies had finally retired as Controller Wales after twenty-two years in the post. There was a new man at the helm, John Rowley, a Montgomeryshire man, a Welsh speaker, who had spent much of his working life in the Consular Service in India before becoming the BBC Controller of Administration. He came to Wales a few months before the new Broadcasting House building was officially opened.

John Rowley had left a central BBC reeling from unexpected changes in its high command. In 1967, Prime Minister Harold Wilson sent shock waves through the organisation with the announcement that Dr Charles Hill was to be the next Chairman of Governors. Dr Hill had been invited to move from his role as Chairman of the commercial regulatory body, the ITA, to take over the BBC. It was an unprecedented action. The Labour

Government had become increasingly irritated by the activities of the BBC, and in particular, of its Director General, the libertarian and adventurous Huw Carleton Greene. The command to Dr Hill, a former broadcaster and a ruthless politician, was 'to sort out the BBC and re-assert the authority of the Governors'. One of his last acts as Chairman of the ITA was to award new commercial television franchises. The tenure for companies such as TWW was ten years, and each one had to re-apply for the right to continue televising for the next ten. The only company to lose its licence in that round of renewal was TWW. At a stroke, that decision changed the image of television in Wales. The new company, called Harlech Television, now HTV, took its name from the Chairman, Lord Harlech. Its board of directors included well-known names: journalist John Morgan; actor Richard Burton; opera singer Sir Geraint Evans, and broadcaster Wynford Vaughan Thomas. Many of the staff whom I had known and worked with at TWW feared for their jobs, as new personnel took over the Pontcanna headquarters. A few senior staff left, others were demoted, but the majority stayed.

It was a strange feeling, going back to the BBC where I began; back to the basics of radio production. There was a new atmosphere, new studios, new technology and a new management. The imposing new Broadcasting House was a statement of the BBC's intent, authority and commitment to Wales. In essence, it was a radio building when it opened in 1967, with one television studio for news and sports programmes, but there was enough land available for further expansion. Television production staff were accommodated in an unprepossessing office building two miles away, not far from the converted chapel studios at Broadway.

No expense had been spared during the building of Broadcasting House in the sixties. It boasted wide, oak-panelled corridors, and offices for managers on the third floor, spacious radio studios and a well-equipped operational centre and presentation area. The air of calm sobriety had been maintained, but we radio people envied the independent attitude, noise and swagger of television people, more especially their stories of wild partying at their club in Newport Road.

My three months as a contract producer passed quickly. New studios, up-to-date equipment and technology made radio production flexible and reactive. There was immediacy too, and contributors from all parts of Wales were able to link up with the main centre in Cardiff, through a network of small studios strategically based in different towns. These were used to obtain immediate reaction from listeners on live programmes, but presenters were given strict guidelines, and warnings not to comment on 'line sound quality' for fear of incurring the wrath of British Telecom.

The equilibrium I had maintained between work and home was upset when an advertisement for the permanent post of General Programmes Producer appeared in the press. The time had come for one of those difficult decisions. Opportunity beckoned, but the practical difficulties and guilt appeared insurmountable. Full-time employment as a permanent staff member seemed problematic and ambiguous. I needed flexible working hours and I needed school holidays. I asked myself repeatedly, did I want to submit myself to the demands of staff regulations plus all those deadlines and responsibilities? David was supportive. The BBC executive was encouraging without being able to give any promises.

Eventually, I persuaded myself to fill in an application form and waited for the outcome.

I was invited for interview. Memories of the last time I faced a BBC interviewing panel came flooding back, as the powerful painting by Kyffin Williams of Controller Alun Oldfield Davies towered on the wall above me. I remembered the feeling of rejection at that time, and the callous excuse, 'needs of the service' for turning me down. This time, I answered cheekily to the question, 'How will you cope?' that my needs were very like the needs of the BBC radio service. The all-male panel didn't blink. They took my concerns seriously; a sign of changing times, and, after consideration, they came to an enlightened decision. I could maintain flexible hours, leaving the building at 3.30 every day; I could take unpaid leave to cover school holidays, and I could remain on contract. I took the job offer at the correct salary, and signed a two-year agreement. I suspect that a measure of flexibility and adaptability proved a turning point for contract staff appointments, although I didn't feel I had in anyway challenged the system. It proved a turning point for me, too. I recognised within myself a need to strike for a measure of independence within my marriage, and a desire to spread my wings and experience.

I was soon in the thick of things. John Rowley invited me to join a committee, chaired by Lorraine, to look at the possibilities of reshaping and restructuring radio in Wales. Network radio had made fundamental broadcasting changes. The familiar Home, Light and Third had metamorphosed into generic networks, Radios One, Two, Three and Four. Wales had been left unfocused and without a sense of direction because much energy and attention had been given to television. New FM frequencies were becoming available, and listening patterns to radio were changing from evening to daytime, as audiences for evening peak-time television viewing soared. The committee was asked to look at ways of maximising the effectiveness of our radio output in Welsh and English. Lorraine was back to her old form: her mind sparking ideas and generating argument and discussion.

First, we looked at wavelengths. Wales had been allocated two broadcasting frequencies, one Medium Wave and one FM. This was the opportunity to separate the two languages into two services on two wavelengths. Two complete national radio services for Wales became more than a gleam in the eye as we began our deliberations. We made our first recommendation. English programmes should be broadcast on Medium Wave and Welsh on FM. Of greater significance, we suggested that they should be broadcast in parallel, at the same time, almost competing with each other. In other words, *Good Morning Wales*, the popular daily topical programme on Medium Wave, should be matched by a new Welsh-language, breakfast programme on FM. Engineering and technology had made it possible. It was up to us now to streamline our resources and to recommend changing working practices.

Within two years, the first Welsh-language breakfast programme, which we called *Bore Da* (Good Morning), became operational from the Bangor production centre. It was an innovative and an exciting step forward. T. Glynne Davies was the ideal presenter; his journalistic style and quirky brand of humour put an individual stamp on the programme and soon endeared him to listeners. His audience increased remarkably. It was enough to kill the notion, put about by sceptics, that a potential audience of half a million Welsh speakers could not sustain a credible and authoritative daily service.

Other issues we tackled involved the range and content of our Welsh programme output, which had languished for some time in the hinterland of our schedules. Audiences for evening transmissions had dwindled. Breakfast, lunch and early evening were becoming peak listening times for radio. We recommended a sharper mix of popular Welsh programmes at 12.30, every day. They included documentaries on contemporary social issues, *Byw a Bod*; a regular discussion series on topical affairs, *Clwb Cinio*; and a sequence of half hour talks/essays by writers on childhood influences, which we called *Llwybrau Gynt*. There were programmes of a lighter vein too, which generated laughter, a commodity that was in short supply on Welsh airwaves of those days. We dreamed up a panel game of words and wit, to be played by two teams of two people, and recorded in village halls up and down rural Wales, which I was invited to produce. The game was endearingly competitive, played by regular team members who were gifted story-spinners, poets, writers and humorists, each one a natural entertainer. Uniquely, the four panel members and the Chairman lived within the boundaries of Cardiganshire, and the special genetic characteristics of that county had given them a wonderful ability to communicate their deep sense of place, identity and roots. Jacob Davies, the Chairman, was a Unitarian Minister and a writer, and the panel members had very different vocations. Cassie Davies was a retired Inspector of Schools, and Marie James kept a village post office and was a County Councillor. Dic Jones and Tydfor Jones were farmers. Both were poets of distinction. Dic had won the chair at the National Eisteddfod, and Tydfor, with his inimitable, eccentric contributions in rhyme and prose, came from a long line of distinguished poets and seafarers. The format that proved so successful on radio was later transferred to television, but as so often happens, not successfully.

Penigamp (Splendid) was a radio programme, its pace and style unsuited to the screen; the panel members looked uncomfortable and they had lost their natural, relaxed manner.

Producing the series was fun and absorbing. I was regularly in the company of poets and writers who interpreted our society in an individual way and could link the cultural values of the past and relate them to the present. It all came to a sudden and brutal end on one January morning, when Jacob Davies died of a massive heart attack. We carried on, but it was never quite the same again.

Because of the committee's deliberations, conformity took a back seat, and we recognised that pop culture was becoming a driving force. Wales shook itself in an attempt to communicate with a young audience. A new pop series was launched, reflecting the music and songs of a new generation of singers led by Dafydd Iwan, Huw Jones and Endaf Emlyn. They were politically engaged in the struggle for the language and independence, and they spoke and sang of a new awakening within young people. The recording industry was growing in significance, and a new radio pop-chart series, making maximum use of new releases, burst on the airwaves on Saturday mornings. Modern, different and relevant, it caught the spirit of the time with its catchy title, *Helo, Sut Dach Chi?* (Hello, How Are You?). Produced by Gareth Lloyd Williams and presented by Hywel Gwynfryn, the series set a tone, and their creative partnership went on to dominate much of Welsh-language broadcasting through the next decade. Other radio producers began to relax into modernity. The highbrow attitude of 'sound broadcasting' was slowly disappearing, edged out by young people influenced by the freedom of the sixties. Our radio production office corridor in Broadcasting House began to echo to the infectious sound of laughter and discussion.

Four

There are moments when every component of your consciousness recognises a turning point. My world crashed one March evening when the daffodils were in full bloom, the tulips were waiting to open, and the young cherry tree was about to burst into glorious pink. We had finished eating supper, and I can still smell the casserole we had eaten. It was spring 1969. This was the evening when David admitted to his on-going affair with another woman. I had felt our marriage had become distant and strained for months and, naively, I believed it was because we were both busy at work. The closeness had gone, the sharing had all but disappeared and he seemed to spend all his time working on a documentary. I was stunned. I knew her; I worked with her. I had introduced them. Once he had blurted out his guilty secret, David got up from his chair as if a wolf pack were at his heels, put on his coat, jumped in his car and roared away, presumably to tell her I knew. Left alone with Huw asleep upstairs, unaware and innocent, I crumbled.

'Easy-to-follow' manuals containing advice on how to cope with situations of deception and marital infidelity were not readily available in those days. I attempted to hide my shame and personal failure under a cloak of respectability — a bit like those huge maternity gowns — but our situation soon became public. Working in the same organisation, the same building, meeting each other 'by chance' in studios and corridors, kept my wounds open and sore, especially when David confessed he could not end the relationship. Within weeks, the situation became intolerable and I asked him to leave. It was a burning of boats situation, but I was angry and desolate, not so much because of her, or at her, but at my own failure. The anger soon turned to darkness and despair, and for months I seemed to roam around robot-like, unable to find solace in sleep or at work. Friends and family were kind and helpful and, for Huw's sake, I tried to keep a semblance of normality, telling him his father was working in London. Of all the expressions of support I received at that time, none was timelier than the action taken by Controller, John Rowley. He did as much as anyone to restore my fragmented ego, ordering me to take a month off work.

'We need you in good heart, we need your skills, and you need time.'

His was an act of managerial kindness and humanity that I appreciated and never forgot.

★   ★   ★

The next paragraphs of this tale cover the period between 1970 and November 1978, when the final separation took place. They are out of sequence within the narrative of this book but I have no wish to dwell in detail on particular events and episodes that finally led to marital breakdown and divorce. A marriage, which had begun with desire and hope, ended in a long-drawn-out saga of unpleasantness and acrimony when I was in my late forties. We could have divorced much earlier. After the initial separation of nine months, I set in motion the process of law, giving adultery as the ground for the marital breakdown. I got as far as the case; Bevan v Bevan was about to be heard in court. As I waited in the anteroom outside the courtroom, the lawyer handling my case, whom I had not met until that afternoon, came in his wig and gown to sit by my side. He told me quietly that I really should re-consider my action. The judge, he said, was a hard man. He would not look kindly on the evidence put before him; he had always made clear in divorce cases that marriage, especially when children were involved, was for life, and that it was obvious, from the documentation, that I had not attempted reconciliation. We talked through my disappointment and confusion. By the end of that session, such was his power of persuasion, I felt flattened and weak. I had no option left; as it seemed to me, sitting in that seedy, stuffy little room, its ashtrays full of cigarette ends and half drunk cups of tea on the table. The law was in command and I was a woman, a chattel. I agreed to try to make the marriage work. The final denouement came as he got up to leave.

'I wouldn't like to see someone like you having to submit to the rigours of questioning in a court room,' he said, and his lips didn't seem to move as he continued, 'I have just spent weeks handling an enquiry on rural development in mid-Wales; your father, as you know, was one of the chief witnesses.' He paused to look around. 'He would not like your marriage to break up without you attempting reconciliation first, would he?'

I had no answer. 'This was the law at work in little old Wales,' I said to myself as I got up to go. My parents had remained supportive but concerned and sad. I walked out of that building in a daze of confused emotions. I was baffled. How had I landed myself in such a situation? I almost felt guilty. My solicitor, who had a reputation as being the best in divorce law, said she too was nonplussed. At the time, this was the only part of her reasoning that seemed to make sense.

We tried reconciliation; we tried almost seven years of it. The gap was too wide, the hurt too deep, the sting of the other woman a constant reminder, so that trust and a close, meaningful relationship became impossible. From my point of view, the situation got worse rather than better. We tried to maintain a semblance of calmness and normality, for Huw, but any feeling of affection that I may have felt at the beginning of the reconciliation years gradually drained away as recriminations and acrimony took over. My marriage was an utter sham. I carried on working; it was only work that gave satisfaction and pleasure. In time, I learnt the art of compartmentalising my mind. I could shut out hurt and unpleasantness; I could also smile, although occasional signs that the other relationship was still intact would cause me to erupt like a firecracker.

After many months of heart searching, I came to the agonising decision that I should walk away from my marriage. David had made it clear that he would not precipitate divorce proceedings, nor would he leave the home. I felt almost like a worn out possession, like an old pair of glasses, the lenses no longer useful to see, and the frames a sign of yesterday's fashion. I was outmoded and I had been out-manoeuvred. It was 1978 and I was appointed Editor Radio Wales, a new job for a new radio service. The future at work was full of possibilities; the future at home was desolate.

Huw was sixteen, and I took the only course of action open to me. It was drastic, maybe unjust, and some would say it was the easy way out, but in an intolerable situation, what constitutes drastic measures appears to make little sense to anyone else. It was rational to the point that I did not ask Huw to come away with me. I left him in his own home, with his father, whom he adored, surrounded by his school friends. To me, it was an attempt to create a life out of a rotten situation. I got on with the job, but it almost broke my heart.

I had found a place to live early in 1978, and when I closed the door on the Pantmawr house for the last time, I felt relief, but the process of buying was not without its difficulties. It soon became obvious that Building Societies considered single women to constitute a high financial risk and women going through a divorce were a race apart. That year, I was fortunate to be appointed to a new job that brought permanent employment and a substantial increase in salary. Eventually, after many attempts had ended in frustration, the Bank agreed to give me a mortgage. As if to underline the difficulties I had encountered, I interviewed the distinguished soprano, Dame Margaret Price, at her home in Paris, and the first question I put to her was, 'Why have you chosen to make Paris your home?'

She replied, 'Simple. No-one in Britain would give me a mortgage. Too much of a risk, they said. I was a single woman in a precarious career, without security, but I was no problem to the French.'

I bought a flat in Llandaff, close to Broadcasting House, and began life as a woman alone. For years, the emotional guilt and the pain would surface unexpectedly, especially the memory of the hurt we could have caused Huw in his growing-up years. David left the BBC for academia; he married and his wife and I continued to circle around each other in the corridors of Broadcasting House. One glorious day, quite soon after they married, Huw, of his own volition, decided to move in with me before going to university. He was supportive of me; understanding was a two-way process as we tried to make sense of the family breakdown.

I became more self-contained as time passed; unable to countenance the possibility of failure from another relationship. I began being me. I had a few flings, nothing more, or as a good friend put it encouragingly, 'You need a good dusting every now and again.'

Carried in the safe hands
of two strong BBC stalwarts
across the flooded showground
at the Royal Welsh Show,
Aberystwyth in 1957.

(Below) Interviewing for a live
television broadcast from the
National Eisteddfod held at
Ebbw Vale in 1958.

T. T. Richards of Llangynwyd was a regular contributor on rural matters for radio and television programmes. Here he brings his skills as a craftsman in the art of hedgelaying to the studio for the news magazine Beunydd.

The Radio Rhondda broadcasting studio all set to go on air at the De Winton car park, Tonypandy in October 1978.

Cliff Morgan and Geraint Stanley Jones celebrating the nomination of the Morning of the Match outside broadcast for a Sony radio award.

Relaxing with renowned tenor Stuart Burrows at the end of his television series.

Checking the Radio Wales schedule on launch day, Monday 13 November 1978. The cleric wearing his Panama is sceptical.

Ken Geen,
Sound Outside Broadcast Engineer,
holds the microphone
to capture an animated
Wynford Vaughan Thomas
as he recalls his experiences
and observations
during his long walk
along The Roof of Wales.

The Seventies

One

The seventies proved to be a decade of political turmoil. The Investiture of the Prince of Wales at Caernarfon Castle in 1969 was the launch pad for sustained controversy and fierce opposition. The event was an anathema to many people and the debate, before and after the ceremony, led to the polarisation of attitudes, not just about the role of royalty in modern Wales, but about the language and the nation as a political entity. Worldwide television coverage had reached over 500 million people. The grandeur of Caernarfon Castle was the perfect theatre for the ceremony but it also symbolised oppression. Cymdeithas yr Iaith Gymraeg (the Welsh Language Society), formed that year, began a vigorous and aggressive campaign to safeguard the language and to counter the decline in the number of Welsh speakers. The influence of television was at the top of their agenda, and the Society pushed for an increase in the number of Welsh-language television programmes and the possibility, as wavelengths became available, for a Welsh-language channel. The BBC in Wales had achieved a degree of autonomy but it was in no position to comply with those demands.

Much of the attention in the early seventies was centred on radio. A wide-ranging internal report called *Broadcasting in the Seventies* had proposed a restructuring and streamlining of all services, networks and regional. Wales and Scotland were to be known as National Regions. Regional radio in England, broadcasting from Bristol, Manchester and Birmingham, was to be dismantled. In its place, the BBC planned to develop local radio stations, especially in cities and urban areas. It was a significant change of emphasis. The English regions had traditionally fed programmes into the network, nurturing writers, musicians and storytellers who, through their work, reflected the diversity and richness of their communities. The decision to centralise radio production of 'high cost' programmes in London gave the networks a metropolitan attitude. Voices and accents reflecting communities north of Watford or west of Windsor were missing from programme schedules, and for a few years in the seventies, the national regions, too, found it difficult to sell their ideas to network controllers.

Another recommendation contained in the report put the BBC Welsh Orchestra in the firing line. It stated the BBC had too many orchestras. They were expensive to maintain and, for that reason, five only would be retained. The Welsh Orchestra, at that time hoping to increase the number of players to attain full symphonic status, was told that additional finance should be sought from other sources. It took two years of vigorous campaigning and a new financial partnership with the Welsh Arts Council to make its future secure.

These issues together with the growing call for a referendum on devolution, came to dominate the lives of broadcasters. In turn, political parties, government agencies, trades unions, institutions and organisations had realised the importance of communicating to a wider public in addition to their members and supporters. The growth of radio news and current affairs programmes at peak listening times punctuated Radio 4 schedules in the early morning, lunchtime and late afternoon. William Hardcastle, the ex-editor of the *Daily Mail*, was brought in to present *The World at One,* and his news sense and hard questioning style gave the programme its journalistic edge and authority.

Wales followed the trend in two languages. Vincent Kane, anchorman of *Good Morning Wales* on Medium Wave, and T. Glynne Davies of *Bore Da* on FM, were different in style and approach but both possessed journalistic credibility and authority. Vincent was the complete broadcaster, a knowledgeable, respected, occasionally feared interviewer by participants on radio and television. Glynne was not as aggressive in tone, yet he was probing and perceptive. The split between MW and FM had been resolved and accepted, and the two early morning magazine programmes, on different wavelengths, began on New Year's Day 1973 but were only operational until nine in the morning. It was a limited service in two languages, a beginning, at the morning peak radio listening time. We used the Radio 4 wavelength at other times in the day and evening to broadcast features, documentaries and discussions in Welsh and English. It was incomplete, messy and frustrating but the pressure for greater autonomy was mounting as the political devolution debate gathered momentum.

The decade was only a year old when there was another managerial upheaval in BBC Wales. Aneirin Talfan Davies, who had led the programme side as Head of Programmes since the death of Hywel Davies, reached the age of retirement. His deputy, D. J. Thomas, was also soon to retire, and this opened up the possibility of appointing a completely new team. Controller John Rowley decided to give himself time to assess likely candidates, although the four he singled out were experienced in production, administration and journalism. He decided to give each, in turn, a period of three months attached to programme management, where he could observe their skills at close quarters. They were Meredydd Evans, the head of Light Entertainment; Alan Protheroe, News Editor; Owen Edwards, Programme Organiser; and Owen Thomas, the Head of Programme Planning and Finance. The bizarre process took a whole year to complete. I suspect the concept had looked promising on paper, but in reality, they roamed the corridors like nomads without portfolio. When the time came for hard-nosed decisions, most of us had put money on our preferred candidate and canteen gossip hardened as the day of decision approached in December.

No sooner had we digested our Christmas dinners than we heard the announcement. It was almost pre-destined. Owen Edwards had been carefully groomed for a managerial role. He had entered broadcasting as a television presenter in the sixties. He had presence and authority and the daily topical magazine programme, *Heddiw*, prospered with him as the front man. He was eventually persuaded to leave his on-screen persona to become an administrator, an organiser in programme planning, and his star was set to shine ever brightly in the broadcasting firmament. Owen came from a distinguished line of educationalists who had a long record in public service. Some called it a Welsh dynasty, and many members of staff were dismayed at his appointment as Head of Programmes, seeing it as proof that the silver-spoon factory had gone into overdrive. He was not known for his creativity, or production and editorial skills, and radio and television needed a strong input of both in the early seventies. It is fair to say that during his tenure we limped along; his inexperience was all too obvious. Then, when John Rowley took early retirement in 1974, Owen was duly appointed Controller and flourished for seven years, his knowledge of Welsh affairs, his gifts as a communicator and public persona bringing authority to BBC Wales at a time of linguistic tensions.

In many respects, the attachment process for the other three candidates had been a bureaucratic, smoke-screened charade. Within months, Meredydd Evans, the enlightened creator of entertainment programmes and a Welsh-language activist, left for academia, and Alan Protheroe joined the news operation in London, where he was to enjoy an illustrious career before becoming Deputy Director General.

It was not all doom and gloom, however. John Rowley and Owen, now acknowledged as his deputy, set about making their own appointments. When D. J. Thomas retired from the post as Assistant Head of Programmes, they selected Geraint Stanley Jones, a young television producer who had a strong record in features and documentaries, and it was he who stepped up to take over the leadership of the programme side when Owen became Controller. The game of hierarchical musical chairs saw the chain of command complete when television producer Gareth Price became the new assistant. The new team was to lead and influence the programme side with vision and organisation for the remainder of the decade. The Head of Programmes was responsible for all radio and television programme output in Wales. By the mid- seventies, it covered some eleven hours of television, six in Welsh and five in English, and fifty hours of radio, twenty in English and thirty in Welsh, in addition to contributions to the radio and television networks.

The issue dominating the headlines remained the issue of television and the Welsh language. Every day, news programmes reflected the mood and events of the time and the growing polarisation of views of communities within Wales. The BBC was accused of giving too much attention to language activists. In the public mind, those views were often confused with the nationalist cause, so much so that a young people's pop television programme, *Disc a Dawn*, and other general interest programmes, were deemed by Labour politicians to be a weekly plug for Plaid Cymru. It also polarised attitudes, and attacks on policy makers became the new sport of the time.

The managerial upheaval of the early seventies crystallised the divisions between those who spoke Welsh and those who did not.

In the BBC, knowledge of Welsh was essential for all senior jobs on the programme side, yet only twenty per cent of the population spoke the language. More money, more hours and more resources were spent on Welsh-language programmes. The BBC saw its public service role as an influential cultural institution to be one of the guardians of the language and to reflect the life of the Welsh-speaking community. Non-Welsh speakers, the majority, believed that argument to be grossly unfair. They were excluded from applying for top programme jobs, and because of a lack of adequate finance the range of television and radio programme activity in English was limited. Arguments on these matters regularly surfaced in the corridors of Broadcasting House, but they lacked the potency and cohesion of the language activists. Cymdeithas yr Iaith had grabbed the headlines, they had orchestrated their protestations and disruption to maximise its effectiveness; they climbed transmitter masts, they disrupted meetings and sat in broadcasting studios and buildings, to ensure maximum publicity. Many were imprisoned for their activities. The argument by the mid-seventies was homing in on the imminent decision to allocate the wavelength for the fourth television channel. Activists and sympathisers believed that by keeping up the pressure they would achieve a Welsh-language television channel.

John Rowley's tenure as Controller spanned the years when the disruptive campaign was at its fiercest, with attacks on studios in Manchester, Bristol, Bush House and a two-day sit-in at Broadcasting House, Llandaff. The strain was too much. He was a man of integrity and his defence of the Orchestra during long deliberations in the higher echelons of the BBC, together with the frustration at not being able to provide a broadcasting solution to the language problem, told on his health. I remember him as a man of humanity who, despite his occasional eccentricities in his dealings with staff, made changes to the programme management team that were to be effective for almost two decades.

While attention focused on television, radio pressed ahead with its own agenda. Lorraine Davies's committee had already seen the possibility of a complete Welsh-language radio service now that the separation of wavelengths was a reality. I had decided at this time to attempt to enter television production. The post of Head of Children's Programmes had become vacant. It was time to have a go. I was a Welsh speaker, I had experience in children's programmes on radio and television, and I was ready for a change. I put in an application and was interviewed rigorously. This time, I was too old. Television was a young man's game and I was the wrong side of forty. The post went to a Young Turk, Dyfed Glyn Jones. I had no quarrel with the appointment; he was a writer and a humorist and soon galvanised the department, but in my mind, ageism had reared its head. I tried for another producer post, in the documentary department. The letter of rejection, without an invitation for an interview, went straight into the bin. I felt it keenly. At forty, I didn't want to become an invisible member of staff, feeling that the best part of my life was over. I think it was my worst disappointment, that feeling of rejection. I remember that I went home to Cardiganshire the following weekend, not to talk, but to walk the familiar fields and to climb the wildness of Mynydd Bach (Small Mountain). From the top, I could see the sweep of Cardigan Bay, the hills of Pumlimon to the north, the mysterious, dark lake of Llyn Eiddwen in front of me, and to the south and east, the patchwork of green fields and woods, the hills and valleys of Cardiganshire and Carmarthenshire. The feelings of rejection and of being under-valued slowly vanished. They seemed to drift silently away on the mountain breezes of the afternoon. It was humbling and I felt chastened that such insignificant reactions should have upset my equilibrium. I was fortunate. I had a job I enjoyed. This was to be a second start. I settled happily for radio, and to this day, I remain satisfied that it was during this time that I did my best work. I had honed my skills and I was confident I could deliver programmes of standard and quality. Motherhood had given me a new and different perspective, training in diplomacy and decision taking, and a troublesome marriage had taught me the value of patience.

The spark of excitement was ignited with the first competition for radio audiences in Wales. The franchise for a new, commercial, local radio station in Swansea had been awarded to a company called Swansea Sound, who promised a 'new dawn' for radio listeners in the area. The BBC had decreed that radio development in Wales should concentrate on national services rather than on setting up local stations. Many communities such as Swansea, with a strong sense of place and identity, disagreed fiercely.

Swansea had been an integral part of the radio system since the first relay station was set up in 1924. Thirteen years later, in 1937, it became a proud production centre housed in a building with modern equipment – 'best in Europe,' so a reporter called it – and furnished lavishly with Brynmawr furniture. Then, in the mid-sixties, with the opening of the new Broadcasting House in Cardiff and an increase in production activity in north Wales, at Bangor, the Controller, Alun Oldfield Davies, saw little need for keeping Swansea open. It was only forty-five miles away from Cardiff, and radio's needs could be best served by keeping a small 'unattended studio' for contributors. Wales, aiming for financial prudence, had caught the centralisation bug. There followed a vociferous campaign, and the staff, confused and angry, were appalled at the decision and never forgave the Controller.

It galvanised our new programme management into action, or at least into thinking seriously about radio's future and the competition we faced. Listening patterns were changing rapidly but, apart from the early morning split of languages on Medium Wave and FM, much of our output, despite dwindling audiences, was broadcast in the evenings. To compete effectively, it was a matter of urgency to widen the scope, nature and scheduling of our programme output.

Geraint Stanley Jones, Assistant Head of Programmes, invited me to deliberate on the possibilities. From that time, the impetus and focus for radio in Wales was challenged and changed.

Two

The trouble with radio in Wales in the early seventies was that it lacked glamour, vibrancy, and creative new ideas; it was cosy and old fashioned. Producers felt comfortable with their old ways, almost afraid of new technology and not keen on making popular programmes. They had never faced the challenge of competition. Now, Swansea Sound was about to open its microphones and no-one quite knew what kind of 'sound' would emerge; it would be a new, bilingual sound for sure, but it was not clear what percentage of its output would be in Welsh and how much in English. Nevertheless, what was very apparent was that a commercially orientated, profit-making station was able to broadcast throughout the day until midnight and appeal to a 'middle of the road' audience. We were being forced to think differently about our production methods and output if we were to make any kind of impact. From the very first 'crystal set' days when radio began in Wales, in 1923, we had been tied to the network UK Home Service, the Radio 4 of today, to broadcast our programmes. The parent service set the tone and style and we followed. Structured, spoken word programmes, of great variety and strength, but since the mid-sixties, peak daytime hours – morning, lunchtime and early evening – they had concentrated on news and current affairs programmes. Our radio programme activity in Wales, at that time named The Welsh Home Service, followed the same pattern.

My musings on the kind of schedule we should aim to achieve suggested we should change the emphasis and think in terms of a lighter, relaxed, more inclusive kind of English programming, widening the appeal. It was pointless contemplating a head-to-head challenge with a local commercial station. We were a national service, but if we were to extend our hours of broadcasting during the day, we needed extra finance. During a visit to Cardiff, the Director General, Charles Curran, took a benign view of our proposals. He realised the competition we faced and decided to allocate an additional sum of money. He was also sympathetic to the notion that Wales should begin planning two national radio services for the future. His reasoning was rather different from ours. He saw it as the answer to the excessive opting out of Radio 4 by the national regions, which was fragmenting the coherence of the UK news and current affairs services.

In a few weeks, I had worked out a programme format; not one to set the broadcasting world on fire and hardly significant enough to compete in any way with the twelve-hour broadcasting days to come from Swansea Sound. It was merely a programme extension of one hour on Monday mornings, immediately following *Good Morning Wales* and the news bulletin at 09.05. Our costs per hour, for one hour a week only, were considerably higher than the costs of a local radio station because we were a national service with different working practices and agreements, plus more complex technology; but at least now, we had the basis for a different daily schedule. I called the weekly series *Nine Five on Monday,* but within six months, we had reorganised and reassessed our finance and resources, and *Nine Five* became the banner title for daily programmes, Monday to Friday.

The format for Monday was simple: a live chat show before an invited audience at Broadcasting House. I had seen how successful the daily record request series *Open House* on Radio 2 was, especially the outside broadcast editions they produced from different locations once a week. These were different, lively, and fun. Conversations with guests drawn from the entertainment scene and the locality took place before an invited audience. The audience reaction to the proceedings gave the programme immediacy and inclusiveness.

I like to think that *Nine Five on Monday* opened the windows of Broadcasting House just a little to the world outside. We involved people, we heard their voices react to issues of the day; it was not a problem or issue-led hour but we gave a fair amount of time to pointed discussion and information. It had a strong show-business element, and that commodity that is always in short supply: the sound of laughter. Each programme was planned carefully and included a star guest from the world of entertainment followed by two local celebrities and dignitaries – never in short supply – from the world of politics, education, sport, media, industry or government agencies. The last fifteen minutes were given over to audience discussion on an issue introduced by reporter, Anita Morgan. Many of my colleagues gasped when they heard I expected to find an audience – and a reactive one at that – to fill Studio 2 at Broadcasting House at nine o'clock in the morning.

It was a challenge but I had convinced myself that it was possible, due mainly, I believe, to my chosen presenter. Wyn Calvin was an entertainer who had begun his career in the Mai Jones era with the successful radio series, *Welsh Rarebit.* Since those days, he had spent his working life in theatres up and down the land, in variety shows, being much in demand as a Dame in countless Christmas pantomimes, but as is often the case with those whose trade is laughter, there is a serious undertone. In addition to knowing everything there is to know about show business, Wyn was well read, accomplished and experienced in radio, and knowledgeable of Welsh affairs. I knew the risk was considerable, but he had the light touch of knowing how to handle an audience, involving them, teasing them and making them feel at ease. His main weakness in the early days was to confuse in his mind the intimacy of the microphone with the larger-than-life theatrical performance. At the time of the first broadcast, Wyn was appearing in a Blackpool summer show and he travelled overnight to Cardiff, to be ready for the nine o'clock deadline. If there were initial faults and stumbling, they were talked about, worked upon and overcome, and as the series continued and developed, Wyn created a niche and a following all his own. It also increased our listening figures, attracting a new audience, which had not turned to BBC Wales for entertainment for many years.

That first programme, broadcast a month or so before Swansea Sound went on air, played into the hands of the doom-laden soothsayers. It was mid-August 1974. Our guests turned up promptly but audience ticket-holders did not. Over 120 tickets had been distributed but only twenty people saw fit to make the effort to attend. I learnt a hard lesson that day: a ticket that costs nothing is worth nothing.

We set about coercing an army of cleaning staff to stay an hour longer at the end of their working shift. Their sacrifice was never forgotten and many were to pay Studio 2 a regular visit on Monday mornings. The numbers for studio audiences grew rapidly. They formed a kind of club, in much the same manner as those who regularly voice their opinions today on telephone lines or e-mails. Many came to see 'in the flesh' the stars from the world of theatre, film and entertainment: Dame Anna Neagle, Dame Flora Robson, Margaret Lockwood, Diana Dors, Sir Geraint Evans, Roy Hudd, Danny La Rue and our first guest, Rolf Harris, who was proud to reveal his family connections with Wales.

We began taking the show on the road and I remember visiting Bangor in North Wales to celebrate the contribution the Penrhyn Hall had made to broadcasting. During the war, the city of Bangor had been home to the BBC's Variety Department, when the production teams were evacuated from London. The Penrhyn Hall was the venue for many variety shows of those years, notably *ITMA* with Tommy Handley. It also played a significant part in Welsh-language light entertainment programmes in the fifties and sixties. Our main star guest that morning in Bangor was the actor Rupert Davies, who played the laid-back detective in the television adaptation of Maigret stories by Georges Simenon. The dangers of producing live shows at five past nine in the morning were never more apparent than when our star guest had not appeared at five to nine. Joan Moody, our researcher, resolute and forthright as ever, ran to the Castle Hotel, disregarded the 'Don't Disturb' notice on the door of Room 2, where the Prince of Wales had once slept, marched in and almost hauled Mr Davies, kicking and bemused, to the Penrhyn Hall.

'And he was wearing red pyjamas,' she said breathlessly as she poured black coffee down the throat of the hung-over actor.

There was a riotous edition from the Adelphi Hotel, Liverpool, with Ken Dodd as star guest; an edgy encounter with the great American film star, Bette Davis, and another, in the concert hall, with comedian Frankie Howerd, when the liquid consumption stretched our budget to its absolute limit.

The edition that had an overwhelming reaction of nostalgia and sentiment came from the Cory Hall, where we gathered a few of those who had performed on its stage. It had been a great temperance hall, a meeting place and a concert hall, and we used the occasion to revive long lost memories of entertainment shows, religious and temperance gatherings, and powerful miners' rallies. The hall's significance to radio audiences was the staging of *Welsh Rarebit* and the long running music series, *Aelwyd y Gân* (Home of Music), presented by Morfudd Mason Lewis and Emrys Cleaver.

The old hall had been condemned to the demolition gangs to make way for a cinema and shopping centre, and our programme was the last function to be held there. The dust and cobwebs were swept away for guests Sir Harry Secombe; miners' leader Dai Francis; broadcaster Alun Williams; playwright and actor Eynon Evans; and the Lyrian Singers, who managed to produce a stirring rendering of the Mai Jones song, *We'll Keep a Welcome*, to open the programme.

The Cory Hall had a wonderful atmosphere and acoustic, but many design faults, as we discovered that morning. Access from one side of the stage to the other was only possible by walking through the auditorium. Dai Francis, third guest on the running order, was seated in a tiny room at the back, listening to the Lyrians singing 'Seventy-six Trombones' (or was it Sixty-Six), when he announced, 'I want the toilet.'

The toilets were to the left of stage. Dai was on the right. Looking after him was the indefatigable Joan Moody, and she was not about to let Dai run cross-legged from right to left in front of the audience. She noticed an old milk bottle on the dusty shelf. The rest is history. Dai was relieved.

When *Nine Five* became a daily event, it became a different programme every day. It included a distinctive record request programme presented by Vince Saville, and I produced a series of live discussion programmes involving sixth-form students. They came from many schools in South Wales, and were invited to share opinions and attitudes on topics chosen by a guest from the world of politics, industry, education and the arts. It was always a robust exchange, and woe betide anyone arrogant enough to dismiss young people as easy fodder. The Rt. Hon. James Callaghan, MP, who was at the time Foreign Secretary, was taxed unmercifully by a group from Atlantic Sixth Form College, who asked about the price of oil and the crisis in Saudi Arabia. He came out of the studio muttering, 'I should never have done that live broadcast. Those youngsters were sharp. Knew what they were talking about and they didn't let go.'

Another political guest, George Brown, Deputy Leader of the Labour Party, arrived in Cardiff after enjoying a good deal of British Rail's liquid hospitality during the journey from London. During the programme, a scholarly boy sitting in the front row doggedly pursued a line of questioning on the use and misuse of power in politics, when George Brown, red-faced, straining every sinew to keep control, suddenly voiced his objection.

'You boy,' he shouted, 'You! You, sitting there comfortably! You're being freely educated. You're wearing your free National Health glasses. What do you know about making decisions in the corridors of power?'

'Not a great deal, Sir, but I'd like to know…'

I forget his supplementary question, but Gerry Monte, the Chairman, kept his cool and gave the eighteen-year-old every opportunity to show his inherent sense of dignity and pride. At the mercy of intelligent young people, the programme often showed the so-called, 'powerful people' as they really were, consumed with their power, occasionally removed from reality, or simply as silly and arrogant. The series eventually transferred to Radio 4 schedules under the title *Sixth Sense*.

The *Nine Five* series reached out to people and involved them. Audience figures went up, but I felt frustrated that we could not extend our broadcasting hours to fill the whole morning. I lived with that frustration for another two years, until the decision taken to establish two national radio services became a reality. In the meantime, I was given another task: to review working practices and programme output from the four major outside broadcast events of the summer. Coverage of our main competitive festivals always dominated the spring and summer schedules. There was the charm of young people at the Urdd National Eisteddfod during the Spring Bank Holiday week; the colour of folk dance and song groups from around the world, at the International Eisteddfod at Llangollen in July; followed by the main Welsh-language National Eisteddfod during the first week of August. In addition, an event close to my heart is the four-day Royal Welsh Agricultural Show, held since the nineteen-sixties at a permanent site at Llanelwedd, Builth Wells, in mid Wales.

Outside-broadcasting equipment was becoming lighter, more flexible, and radio microphones had widened the range, but our programme coverage was moribund, confined to old ways, mainly recording programme material during the day and broadcasting highlights in the evenings. Much of our engineering effort was misdirected. Technology and production organisation could allow listeners to enjoy proceedings direct and uninterrupted from festival venues during the day, which would at least maximise the considerable investment and outlay such expensive outside broadcasts involved.

I put ideas into practice at the 1975 National Eisteddfod, held that year at Cricieth. For the first time, listeners enjoyed extended coverage of proceedings, with commentary, from the Eisteddfod stage. It brought immediate reaction and appreciation.

Being part of something new and witnessing ideas developed on paper turn into live reality is a joy. Success is a bonus. It can only happen when the team is enthusiastic and has adventurous production skills. Gareth Lloyd Williams, the producer, and Hywel Gwynfryn, the presenter, formed a creative partnership, and daytime radio broadcasting in Wales took a giant step forward at Cricieth. They set the tone and the style for Welsh-language broadcasting for the next two decades, and the pattern of radio coverage of summer events has remained to this day.

I took the same principle to the Royal Welsh Show. Coverage of different events on the huge showground was difficult and static, until I happened to see a piece of equipment used for the first time to cover the Open Golf tournament in Scotland. It was a small transmitter with a range of five miles, carried in a kind of haversack. Attached to the transmitter was a microphone. I asked London engineers whether I could borrow it for the agricultural show. The 'back pack', as it was called, was simple, effective and immediate. Presenters and reporters were no longer tied to one spot; it allowed them to walk and talk and to broadcast interviews and impressions from all areas of the show ground. It transformed our coverage. Listeners were there, in the middle of it all, capturing the atmosphere.

These additional technical resources had given outside broadcasts another dimension, but there remained the more traditional coverage of broadcasting highlights and assessing a day's proceedings. A week-long National Eisteddfod, held at a different location every year, was a huge undertaking for radio and television. I produced the evening 'pull-together' programme called *Tocyn Wythnos* (Weekly Ticket) for three years, which meant listening to the day's output from the Pavilion stage, competitions and ceremonies, together with the various reports and activities from different events taking place in other, smaller pavilions on the Eisteddfod field. To spend a hot day closeted in a small studio, collating and editing material to fill a nightly hour and half of programme time, beginning at 7.30 p.m. could be sticky, irritating and tiring. It was an early start and a late finish but there were compensations. Working with Carwyn James at the Cardigan National was one. It was 1976, that long, hot summer when our studio campus became a thirst-quenching watering hole for the cultural glitterati. The Eisteddfod operates a rigid non-alcohol policy, but that year, Carwyn and I carried gallons of more potent liquid – Carwyn's favourite tipple – onto the field, and placed it in the bottom drawer of an unprepossessing steel filing cabinet. There was often a queue outside the door as poets, writers and musicians came for their daily, creative, intoxicating, 'fix' from something stronger than water. The Nonconformist hypocrisy on temperance matters such as the 'evil of drink' went out with the bath water during that hot week.

Carwyn was known internationally as an icon of rugby, especially following his work as a coach to the British Lions and the rare victory in 1971 over New Zealand, but in addition to his exploits on the rugby field, he was known as a teacher and lecturer, a politician, a writer and broadcaster on Welsh affairs. He held an unique position in Welsh life. I worked with him on a wide range of programmes, and I would often be invited for Sunday lunch at his family home in Cefneithin, where his mother and sister, Gwen, served Welsh lamb and fresh vegetables from the garden followed by apple tart and cream. They never once ate with us at table. It was not the custom. They took pleasure from seeing their men and guests well fed and content. They usually ate before we did. Carwyn was an indulged favoured son and brother, I was often an unexpected guest, but they would sit in armchairs, Gwen and her mother, on either side of the fire while we ate, and slowly relate the happenings of the week in the world of Cefneithin village.

Carwyn died tragically and suddenly of a heart attack, in Amsterdam in 1983. The night before his death, he telephoned me, his last call, to enquire how the Llanelli rugby teams had fared in the Welsh cup tournament. He was an inspirational coach to the west Wales team, and when I told him that it was a drawn game, he said,

'I'll be back on Monday. I'll analyse the tape then.'

His funeral, delayed because of organisational regulations, took place the same day as we buried my father. It was a sad time.

The hot summer of 1976 by no means scorched the will and determination of broadcasters to establish two fully-fledged radio services. The spirit of devolution was in the air. Politicians were heeding the pressure for Wales and Scotland to have greater autonomy over their affairs. There was talk of assemblies and parliaments as the Labour Government began the long consultation process on devolution before holding a referendum on the issue. Against this background, the BBC recognised that it, too, should bow to demands from the national regions. The case for national radio services became a pressing issue, and I well remember a significant discussion when Douglas Muggeridge, then Director of Radio, came to Cardiff to declare that London had earmarked money to appoint nine extra producers for Wales. It seemed the heavens were about to open and rain gold coins upon us. However, it was not to be. When the referendum votes were counted, devolved power had been rejected by a considerable margin. The radio directorate in London breathed again and the money was diverted elsewhere, and I guess the concept of financing nine producers suffered a melt down. I suppose it was the first time I came to realise how fickle promises by London's radio directorate could be, and how deep the differences really were. We were rarely regarded as equals.

Three

One of the hazards of programme-making is determining the ownership of an idea. The rules governing copyright on formats and programme material are well documented but they can become confused and difficult to define when more than one person is involved. I became involved in just such a legal issue in the mid-seventies. John Crosby levelled a charge against me for not acknowledging publicly and financially a programme idea for a series that I produced and that he maintained was his.

I had met him when he came to take part in a *Nine Five* discussion on loneliness. Claire Rayner, the *Sun* agony columnist, was our chief guest, and John Crosby, a recent divorcee bringing up two teenage children, was an effective contributor. When transmission ended, the discussion continued and Claire, as ever, was involved and patient. As we left the studio, she said, 'Perhaps you and I could mount a whole series of programmes on loneliness.'

John Crosby followed us to the canteen for coffee, and it became clear he was anxious to become involved as a broadcaster; in fact, after that encounter, he often telephoned, but I could offer him little at that stage. Claire and I went on to elaborate on the initial idea, and gradually a programme format, which we titled *Contact*, emerged from our discussions. It involved interviewing on air people who admitted to being lonely, exploring their circumstances and discovering how they were attempting to cope. The hope was that others in a similar position would make contact after listening to the programme. The interviewees would not be named during the broadcast, and confidentiality was maintained throughout the process. The programmes became reasonably successful but from some quarters came accusations of voyeurism. The most satisfying reaction to the series was that we were able to set up a number of Contact clubs for lonely people.

Following the first transmission, I received a letter from John Crosby, stating that the format was his, that he had put forward the idea, and that unless he was recognised publicly as the originator, and a royalty fee agreed, he would involve the law. His submission was totally incorrect. There was no question of an agreement between us. John Crosby took the matter to court and decided to defend himself. I had the support of the BBC's legal department and the clear and objective approach of Cardiff solicitor, Michael Petersen. He became a good friend, and I came to rely on him for his wise counsel during the 'low days'. After hearing evidence from both sides in a case that took two days to complete, the Judge ruled against the charge. I was innocent, but the experience of being in a courtroom, of giving evidence, of being questioned in the witness box, and the publicity surrounding the case provided me with another bruising. The isolation I felt at a most vulnerable time, at home, and from a few senior colleagues, when my integrity and truthfulness came into question, was painful. Luckily, the case ended, a few hours, in fact, before I headed for Heathrow and my first visit to the USA, in December 1977.

I had been planning the visit for months, in conjunction with the Wales Tourist Board. It was a bus tour, taking in key resorts on the East Coast, from Washington to Miami. The Chairman of the Board, Lord Gordon Parry, suggested that joining such a tour would enable me, at a reasonable cost, to make radio programmes about tourism and other subjects and topics of interest to listeners in Wales. Surprisingly, my superiors agreed; and the care shown by Gordon and his wife, Glenys, helped me during the following fortnight to overcome the public hurt of the court case and the angst in my private life.

I had arranged many meetings and interviews before leaving Cardiff, taking full advantage of the many stopovers during the journey from north to south. At dawn on the first morning, after landing in Washington, I took a fast taxi around government buildings in Washington and Capitol Hill before catching the train to Baltimore, where I was to meet a remarkable lady.

Amy Evans from Tonypandy was well into her nineties. At the age of twenty, she had the distinction of being the youngest soprano to win the open competition at the 1898 National Eisteddfod in Cardiff. She went on to carve a successful professional career, eventually marrying and making her home in the States. That December morning, when I met her in her Baltimore apartment, she sat regally in a high-backed chair, surrounded by acres of photographs and memorabilia, recalling a glittering past and every precise detail of one amazing day in Wales seventy years earlier. She told me about the kind patronage of the Countess of Plymouth, the support of parents and siblings, the clothes she wore, the heat and nerves of the prelims in the morning, the performance in the afternoon, and the roar of approval from the huge audience when the adjudicator declared, 'The winner is Amy Evans from Tonypandy'. The story took exactly twelve minutes to tell, and as the recording tape was about to finish, her eyes glistening with tears, she said, 'It's a day I'll never forget. The valleys sang with me that day.'

Amy Evans was content with her memories; for me it was a rare insight into life in the valleys, into the kind of patronage offered by the gentry at the turn of the century, and the fact that I could capture it all on tape was a delight.

Amy Evans was a performer and a master storyteller, and I encountered many others during the fourteen-day journey. We travelled through the well-preserved town of Williamsburgh, the developing resort of Myrtle Beach, sampled the distinctive atmosphere and deep south architecture of Savannah, and the twentieth-century Disney wonderland in Orlando. Almost at the end of the trip, there remained one star interview to record. The entertainer, Cardiff-born Tessie O'Shea, was coming to the end of her flourishing career as Two Ton Tess, and had decided to settle and retire at Ocala, north Florida; she had agreed to be interviewed.

Gordon insisted on coming with me. 'Can't go on your own,' he said.

We hired a large brown Oldsmobile at Daytona Beach and made our way across the state. Gordon drove like a bat out of hell down the highway, and, after the first thirty minutes, we were puzzled when every approaching vehicle frantically flashed lights and waved at us.

'They must know the Lord is coming,' said Gordon, before pulling off the road to investigate. The Oldsmobile was lit up like a Christmas tree: winkers, headlights, fog and hazard lights were dazzling in competition with the Floridian sun. Later, when we stopped for lunch, the safety and siren system became operational, and a horn deep in the car's engine warned us not to open the doors. We were too afraid and too stiff to make a run for it. A young girl, no more than fifteen years old, sauntered across.

'You guys got trouble?' she asked. She was a Rita Hayworth look-alike. 'I'll fix it,' she said and, with a flick of the wrist, she did. 'You guys enjoy your lunch.' Whereupon she sauntered off with the poise of a film star, too.

Tessie had a larger-than-life reputation, but the first impression of her home was of an unassuming and undistinguished two-storey, brown, wooden building hugging the side of a quiet country road. It had once been a village store. We walked along the path to the garden at the back and there, almost hidden from view, was Tessie, dressed simply in a free-flowing dress, straw hat perched on her blonde hair, singing quietly to herself while she raked leaves from under the trees in the orange grove. 'Hello, darlings,' she greeted us, her smile as warm as the sun. 'You found me.'

It was a visit tinged with sadness, and the memory has stayed vividly in my mind ever since. The vivaciousness and the warmth of her bubbly character, which had always been the hallmark of her performing personality, had become a cover for loneliness. She had found herself sharing her home, for whatever reason, with her musical director and his young family. Tessie lived in a poky little room below stairs, while the family lived above, in more spacious accommodation.

We followed her around the narrow, dark passages while she talked. She came to a door and her face lit up.

'Look, there it is. My pride and joy,' and she lifted a covering to reveal a large black Daimler car in pristine condition. 'I had it shipped over specially. Oh, darlings, if it could talk, it could tell you lots.' Her hand caressed the bonnet, 'I'm keeping it under wraps,' and she smiled her toothy smile, 'just like me…' she paused theatrically, 'for now!'

The storage area around the car was piled high with packing boxes. Tessie's life was unopened in the darkness.

She was pleased to see us. She wanted to hear about Wales and Cardiff. She told us of her childhood and family in the city, her great days in vaudeville and films, the vicissitudes of a life in entertainment but, loyal to the end, she remained tight-lipped about her present circumstances. There was pride and dignity but I'm sure longing and great sadness were never far away. My interview and the programme respected her feelings.

I had always found pleasure in music without in any way being knowledgeable. Working with the Orchestra for Children's programmes had given me an insight into great classical works. I had loved the range and panache of the colourful American musical shows such as *Oklahoma, Carousel*, and *South Pacific*, and no Welsh person could fail to sing (in four parts, of course) arias from the great religious oratorios. I was introduced to opera and the Welsh National Opera productions in the seventies, and I soon became entranced with the staging and singing of operas such as *Nabucco, Madame Butterfly* and *Eugene Onegin*. The company was gaining international recognition under the guidance of the youthful partnership of Richard Armstrong, Musical Director, and Brian Macmaster, the Managing Director; and hearing some of our greatest singers in WNO productions were occasions to treasure. I got to know many of them as friends and came to realise how singers in opera, blessed with the ability to stir the most fundamental emotion and admiration, often live on a knife-edge of concern for the fragility of their voices.

I began a series called *A Musical Evening,* which found a place in Radio 4 schedules for a number of years. At the time, prestigious international opera houses recognised the wonderful singing of great Welsh singers such as Sir Geraint Evans, Stuart Burrows, Margaret Price, Gwyneth Jones and Gwynne Howell. These hour-long programmes gave them an opportunity to talk about their careers and their technique, and explain how they interpreted favourite roles. The interviews were illustrated with recorded arias, but the series began in a very different way.

We had mounted an edition of Wyn Calvin's *Nine Five* from the community hall at Cilfynydd, twelve miles from Cardiff. Amazingly, four celebrity guests had roots deeply embedded in that small mining village. Tenor Stuart Burrows, like Geraint Evans, was born and brought up in William Street. Others from the village who sat on the platform that night were Geraint's brother-in-law, Glyn Davies, the mercurial International rugby fly half of the forties, who became Managing Director of a large wine business in Bristol; the Rt. Hon. Merlyn Rees, MP, who was the Labour Government Secretary of State for Northern Ireland; and Trevor Davies, the BBC's long-serving television weatherman. When we completed the programme, Stuart and I continued to discuss the demise of the old valley communities. Coalmining was an industry in rapid decline, although no-one could have foreseen how, six years later, those communities were ripped apart during the miners' strike, with the publication of plans to close every coal mine in South Wales. After the programme, Stuart looked hard at William Street and saw that a Chinese takeaway had replaced the village shop, and Bethel chapel, where he had learnt to sing as a child, had closed its doors for good.

We could just about see inside the building through a dirty cracked window, and it seemed to be bereft of a soul. The organ, which had never really seen good days, was a forlorn sight. Undeterred by such small inconveniences, Stuart felt the place should have 'one last chance, one last concert'. He would sing in the chapel where he had started on the road to operatic fame. He set about persuading me to record a concert he had agreed to give in the village to raise money for old age pensioners.

'This is the right venue,' he said, his voice shaking with excitement. 'Bethel will come alive again. Just like the old days.'

I bowed to the enthusiasm. We took out the *Sêt Fawr*, the Big Pew, where Bethel deacons had sat listening to powerful sermons, and wheeled in a hired grand piano to take its place. From early morning, the piano tuner worked at the notes, while local ladies brushed, dusted and polished until the pews and aisles gleamed. A constant supply of tea and Welsh cakes kept the men happy as they checked every seat and light bulb and debated who was to be doing what when the doors opened at 7.15 for the concert to start at 8 o'clock prompt. The chapel was full to capacity by 7.40, the anticipation tangible, the atmosphere electric, the gallery almost sagging under the weight of bodies. Stuart performed a miracle. He sang arias from operas and oratorios, old Victorian songs and stirring Welsh ballads and, best of all, he sang some of the old Welsh hymns as encores. Not even the great religious revival of 1904 had witnessed such an evening, so charged with emotion. He talked of his childhood, he told stories of his travels and of his experiences in the great opera houses of the world. Condensation flowed down the walls and windows, but nobody wanted to go home, and they stayed, begging for encores, until well past 11 o'clock. At midnight, the lights went out for the last time, but the chapel had played its part in raising enough money to restore a worthy centre for the Cilfynydd old age pensioners.

Complex outside broadcasts take stamina and organisation to arrange and are often limited in their appeal. The audience listening at home is unable to become involved in the broadcast. Not everyone has Stuart's gifts of being able to talk and sing with such ease before an audience, and I changed the nature of *A Musical Evening* into interviews and recorded music. All the leading Welsh singers agreed to take part and, as the months passed, I invited the most talented of producers, Mark Owen, to take charge of production. He was a Rhondda boy, an Oxford graduate, who had a prodigious knowledge of opera and singers, and he extended the range of guests and the style of questioning. We talked to leading international singers such as Thomas Allen and Renata Scotto, we visited Barcelona to interview Montserrat Caballe, Teresa Berganza and Alfred Krauz, and we went to New York to meet Tatyana Troyanos, Grace Bumbry and Roberta Peters.

A chance meeting with Wynford Vaughan Thomas at a function took me in a very different direction. During our talk, I reminded him of a two-hundred-mile broadcast walk he had undertaken twenty years earlier, to celebrate his fiftieth birthday. He had been one of radio's most illustrious war correspondents, and despite his work as Director of Programmes with HTV, he had continued to present BBC radio programmes, and to be a leading commentator at great royal events. During our conversation at that chance meeting, he told me he was about to retire, and immediately I suggested he might like to repeat the walk the following year, 1978, to celebrate his seventieth birthday. He didn't need to be persuaded, the challenge appealed, and he agreed almost at once. In addition to all his broadcasting gifts, the breadth of his knowledge, his commitment to environmental causes, and his sense of heritage and continuity, his enthusiastic zest for life and people endeared Wynford to everyone.

The challenge, a huge undertaking, was a walk over some of the roughest terrain in Wales, from Port Talbot in the south to Penmaenmawr in the north, over two hundred miles, to be completed, for broadcasting purposes, in nine days. The route, which Wynford devised, was called *The Roof of Wales*. In essence, it took him along the spine of Wales, marking the mountain sources of the great rivers, those that flowed to the east such as the Severn and the Wye, and those to the west, the Towy and the Teifi.

We planned and plotted meticulously for months, during which Wynford followed a rigorous training schedule on his beloved Preseli hills in Pembrokeshire, and I spent the time on more mundane logistical matters. We were a team of three. I chose as my engineer Ken Geen, the most unassuming of men, but the most skilled outside-broadcast engineer and a creative tape editor. This was a rare combination in any radio era, and not once in all our journeys together did he become flustered with his machines, or lose his cool at my demands. The BBC at that time had so many jewels like Ken but failed to find a way of rewarding them adequately for the brilliance of their contribution to programme-making. Madeleine, my PA, took care of practical matters, always 'fixing' the impossible, and was the catalyst for so much wit and laughter during many frustrating and tiring days. We were the back-up team, who watered and fed Wynford during the twenty-mile walking days, recording interviews, editing tape and ensuring each completed daily programme reached Cardiff by motorbike in time for transmission at five past nine the following morning. It was a tight schedule and a challenge, but achievable.

The weather was sunny and hot in mid-June, when Wynford crossed the M4 at Port Talbot and headed for the hills for his marathon endurance test. Four hours later, he had reached the high vantage point of the *Bwlch* above the Rhondda valleys, and stopped to share a sandwich lunch and to record an interview with the writer and humorist, Gwyn Thomas. Perspiration caused by heat and exertion had flowed through swathes of sun cream on his face, until Wynford's eyes looked like two pink beacons. Gwyn looked at him.

'I don't believe in lotions, Wynford,' he paused dramatically, 'only liquids... em, of the right kind.' Gwyn drank deeply from our bottle of Bells.

Wynford followed his strict diet regime as he walked over the Breconshire Fans and the Epynt, before approaching the vast emptiness of the Cambrian hills of mid-Wales. It was there, on the fourth day of walking, that disaster very nearly put a stop to the project. He was late arriving at our pre-arranged meeting place above the remote Teifi Pools, causing the local forester waiting to be interviewed to say prophetically, 'I'll give him a bollocking for doing this on his own.'

Worse was to follow. At the last pre-arranged meeting place of the day, high above the village of Cwmystwyth, Wynford was seriously late. He had calculated, usually correct to within fifteen minutes, that he would arrive at five in the afternoon, before walking the final hop, to bed down at the Eisteddfa Gurig hostelry on the foothills of Pumlumon. We waited, we scanned the hills for signs of movement, and we became agitated. Almost four hours went by and the two men who had joined us to be interviewed, Llewelyn Phillips, the writer and scientist, and Moc Morgan, world-renowned angler and schoolteacher, who knew the terrain well, became seriously concerned. Soon, they said, the light would fail and I would have to face the inevitable. It was cold comfort, but Wynford was lost in the hills. Madeleine plied them with sandwiches, and the bottle of Bells slowly emptied. I sped to the nearest farmhouse and the nearest telephone, two miles away, to speak to my bosses and to the police.

Within minutes of my returning to join the others, we heard the roar of a car speeding up the valley's narrow road, headlights at full strength, to stop dramatically next to Ken's Landrover. Out of the Mini stepped a resplendently uniformed, peak-capped Superintendent of Police, followed by a constable. There followed a methodical question-and-answer session, and a look of incredulity settled on their faces as I explained the project and reported on the happenings of the past few days. They were obviously not radio listeners, but the Superintendent's countenance beneath the peaked cap quickly implied that an organisation like the BBC should not have allowed a seventy-year-old gentleman to undertake such a dangerous escapade.

'I fear the worst.' His deep bass voice resonated in the silence of the gloom. 'We will do our best now, but the full search will have to wait until first light tomorrow morning.' He pulled himself to his full height of authority to address the constable.

'O'Reilly,' he commanded, 'see that hill in front of you?'

'Yes sir.' The Irish youngster clicked his heels to attention, and a couple of ewes ran for cover.

'I want you to march to the top. Scan the horizon. See if you can see Mr Wynford Vaughan Thomas. He was last seen wearing a light-green anorak, a red bobble hat and army trousers.'

Llewelyn muttered knowingly, 'He'll stand out from the sheep.'

'O'Reilly! March!'

O'Reilly marched upwards, straight backed and unbending, to the top. We watched in silent wonderment. Surely, the robust Irishman would divine Wynford from the bleak hills. I felt a hand grip my arm. It was the Superintendent, who drew me aside, away from the others, to whisper, 'Mrs Bevan, you make radio programmes, don't you?' I nodded. His face came closer, 'I'm secretary of the Aberystwyth Male Voice Choir and they've never been invited to sing on radio. How's it looking?'

I was face-to-face with the subtle art of networking and influencing within the law. Before I could reply, we heard a voice calling, 'Hello, anyone there? Sorry I'm late.'

Wynford appeared, tired but safe, after walking over forty miles. He had misread his new Swedish compass somewhere deep in the desert of Wales. He had turned to the east instead of west, only realising his mistake when he saw the huge Claerwen dam. We bundled him in the car and made for the hostelry, but the owners of the establishment had omitted to tell us they were hosting a young farmers' barn dance that night. The place was alive with the sound of music, whooping voices and flashing lights. It was also the week of the 1978 World Cup, and, in a small back room where two old shepherds sat glued to the television, watching a kicking match between Argentina and Uruguay, we recorded Wynford's recollections of his adventures. They didn't mind the sound being turned down. They grinned.

'After all, it's not Wales, is it?'

However, the day was not done; there was yet another mishap to overcome. Ken Geen's Landrover, our studio and workshop, developed a puncture on the way to our hotel, three miles away, where we were to edit the tapes. Eventually, after many stop-starts, the completed programme left for Cardiff at four in the morning.

I'm sure it was mind over matter that kept a tired Wynford walking the following day. At the end of it, he summoned the last ounce of energy for the recording at our next over-night stop, the Black Lion, Llanbrynmair. We had almost finished when the door slowly opened and in walked athlete, mountaineer, environmentalist and journalist, Chris Brasher, and his friend Johnny. They had listened to the programme that morning in London and had immediately driven to Wales to assist their friend, and to accompany him for the next four days. They knew the mountains of North Wales well, the risks were great, and they had brought with them a new pair of light-weight, sturdy boots – a pair of wings, as Wynford called them – and another compass.

It was a memorable company. We were now in safe hands as the walk continued over the Aran, the Carneddau and the Snowdonia mountain ranges, before reaching Penmaenmawr on the eve of the ninth day. A large crowd had gathered to meet them and to applaud Wynford's feat of stamina and endurance. They were his listeners and admirers who had followed the journey by listening to the daily reports on radio. On our way, by car, to the last hotel, Wynford and I stopped at a wayside inn for a quiet celebratory drink together. He lifted his glass; the eyes twinkled.

'Seventy in August. I don't feel it.'

We accomplished two more long journeys through Wales, both on horseback. Wynford was not a natural equestrian but he was brave. Diligent training in the saddle on a Welsh cob called Toby gave him a modicum of confidence. His observations and reporting skills coupled with his passion for history, the countryside and environmental issues touched a chord with the audience. Invariably, people wanted to talk to him and he, in turn, relished the contact. I can remember well a few locals standing at the bar in the Castle Hotel, Merthyr Tydfil, and encouraging Wynford at the beginning of his ride along the borders of Wales, to wear a pair of women's tights under his trousers in order to avoid chafed skin in tender parts.

Wynford pooh-poohed the idea, but the men pressed home their local knowledge. 'All the mountain riders around here wear them. It's true,' they said as our faces reflected our scepticism, 'and there's nothing wrong with the men.'

Madeleine was despatched to find a pair 'without seams and not fishnets, remember'.

He wore them for exactly one hour the following day, and never once in nine days did he complain of soreness.

I made many other documentaries with him. A series recalling some of his memorable war experiences included a visit to the Anzio beachhead, where he was reduced to tears when walking the waddies, picking up bits of shrapnel, and visiting the graves of young men in the military cemetery. We flew over Berlin, recapturing, with recordings he made at the time, the flight with Bomber Command on a mission to flatten the great city. These were programme-making experiences of brilliant story telling; his company and his intellect brought a sparkle to every conversation.

Nevertheless, there were tantrums too. Then, there was the added complexity and duplicity in his private life, which he carried off with the innocence of a child, as though he had stumbled into a situation not of his making. He walked the tightest of tightropes. Lotte, his wife lived in Fishguard, and Enid, his companion during his more public role as Director of Programmes, lived in Swansea. Enid once declared that she would like to ride with him on one of the radio journeys. I needed no time to consider. I told him we had contracted to look after *one* horse for nine days. Two horses was one too many. The relief was palpable. It had been a narrow escape, but the relationship survived, and he could now blame me for banning her.

When the cancer struck, he was angry but not once during the long months of pain and treatment did he lose the capacity to generate goodwill and laughter. He looked forward and he kept alive his concerns for the landscape he cherished, the environment he treasured, and the nation that at times exasperated but always inspired him.

Four

Two national radio services for Wales became a reality in 1978. Radio Wales was born and I became its first editor. The opportunity to structure and establish a new network does not often occur, and the six months between April, when I heard I had been appointed, and the launch in November, were full of activity, excitement, and more than a little apprehension. I was now a member of the senior programme management team, and, within days, I realised that the position of a manager and an editor immediately set me apart from the pack. I accepted the challenge but not without some initial misgivings. I was a 'hands on' programme-maker, and the time to adjust into a new managerial role and all that it entailed was a mere six months. The position carried a higher salary, and the designated office was slightly larger, albeit six doors up from my present one. I was also entitled to have curtains on the windows, a better quality carpet on the floor, a different colour on the walls from the regulatory Barley White, and a small fridge.

Two editorial posts were advertised, although the Welsh-language service would not become operational until the following year. I would have been content to be offered either post: to lead the Welsh-language service, Radio Cymru, or Radio Wales, the English service, but the interviewing board decided that although I was a Welsh speaker I should edit Radio Wales. Until these posts were advertised, all senior positions in the programme establishment made the ability to speak Welsh a compulsory requirement. Radio Wales was open to competition from non-Welsh speakers. As soon as news of my appointment became public, hostilities began. A few colleagues I had considered close friends felt that, by taking the English post, I had abandoned, even betrayed, the cause of the Welsh language in broadcasting. Worse, I would be working in direct competition for listeners when both networks became operational.

Others complained that I could not possibly know, or reflect, the opinions and attitudes of the non-Welsh-speaking majority who, down the decades, believed that the BBC establishment in Wales had disenfranchised them. The linguistic divisions and resentments of the seventies turned into open combat within the walls of Broadcasting House. I began to doubt my capabilities and skills, and to ask myself why I had agreed to take on the job, but the challenge was irresistible. It was an opportunity to create for the first time a radio service that would give Wales a national forum and identity. Radio Cymru, the Welsh-language service, also faced the challenge of building a schedule to attract a new audience.

The radio-programme establishment was small, but when we had completed our recruitment, a new generation of young producers brought with them new attitudes and fresh ideas. The potency of old enmities was, for a period, blunted.

Time was short to prepare and plan in readiness for the launch date of 13 November 1978. Thankfully, it was not a Friday, but the date had been chosen to coincide with the launch of Radio Scotland and Radio Ulster. The pressure for devolution in the nations had worked wonders in forcing the BBC centrally to release the necessary funding. My head was full of programme ideas, staffing structures, budgets, and one weekend in early May, we sat down to work out the practical financial and resource needs for the expansion.

I wanted to create a more inclusive and relevant channel, one which was accessible and interactive. Generic UK radio networks 1, 2, 3 and 4 divided and categorised audiences. Traditionally, Wales had opted out of Radio 4, and our programmes adopted the tone and style of the channel but, excellent as it was, with the dominance of news and current affairs, the network's audience at that time was falling. This was an opportunity for Radio Wales to stand alone and to create its own schedule, free of opting out of another channel, and to be more popular in character. The challenge for me was to attract new listeners. The disenfranchised majority would no longer to be known as the Anglo-Welsh; they were Welsh.

As a first outline of a daytime schedule, I included an emphasis on longer sequences of programmes based on a mix of speech and music and the personality of presenters. Operational areas and old working practices were transformed, and many presenters were required to learn new skills, such as operating studio equipment, in order to put themselves on air.

Three senior producers were the first appointments, my next in line of command, to lead three production units. They were different in character and style. David Nicholas was given the task of shaping a new early morning sequence. He was an experienced journalist, quirky, occasionally stubborn, but brim full of ideas. Dewi Smith was widely experienced in current affairs, keenly interested in music; a solid programme-maker, he took on the additional responsibilities for creating a variety of morning programme sequences. I had already determined that the sequence around lunchtime, at noon every day, should be speech-based. Gareth Rowlands took on the task of creating a framework for the slot. In addition, he devised the title, *Meet For Lunch with Vincent Kane*. The three senior producers were in their thirties, experienced radio practitioners and, like me, Welsh speaking, reflecting the BBC Wales profile of the time.

The next appointments – producers and researchers – changed the linguistic balance. The advertisements had generated interest from hundreds of applicants, and those selected were young and different, mostly in their twenties, the majority non-Welsh speakers. One or two had worked in local radio and other closely related jobs; a few were recent graduates who found themselves on the threshold of careers in broadcasting. Sensitivities concerning the language issue were never far away. We selected Vaughan Roderick as one of the researchers. He was in his early twenties, lively, interested in politics and Welsh affairs, a language activist and a member of Cymdeithas yr Iaith Gymraeg (the Welsh Language Society). During one of their campaigns, he had been arrested and charged. A member of the Broadcasting Council disagreed strongly with the appointment, taking the view that the BBC should not employ a person who had broken the law. Vaughan had promised, during his interview, not to continue being politically active, and he joined Radio Wales, where he was to make a significant contribution. I refused to budge on the issue, and Vaughan turned his political campaigning to practical advantage by establishing a five-minute, daily learning-Welsh lesson called *Catchphrase*. He and presenter Dan Damon, who had joined us from London, worked together on a morning record request programme, and they decided Dan would have an on-air Welsh lesson every morning. His progress and his difficulties could encourage listeners to join him. Cennard Davies, a brilliant teacher and enthusiast, prepared five-minute lessons, and within a few months, such was the interest, they were able to hold social gatherings at different locations for 'learners' to share experiences. It was an unqualified success. Preparing back-up notes and informative packs about the language became an industry. Within a year, Dan had mastered the intricacies of the language in a most public way. He left Wales to continue his career in television and network radio, but not before his children had also learnt Welsh in school. Vaughan remains as a robust current affairs presenter and a political correspondent.

Working to an overall brief, the production units set to work on ideas and programme structures unfettered by old-fashioned techniques and attitudes. The style and tone of the new Radio Wales was to be different and distinctive. Attempts to define that aspiration settled on the description 'Radio Two and a Half'. The nine producers and five researchers quickly bonded into a vibrant team but, within weeks, I came into direct confrontation with journalists working in news and current affairs. They disagreed with the overall plans and they certainly opposed any change involving what they believed was their territory, and *Good Morning Wales* in particular. Gareth Bowen, who edited the programme and who had lost the editorship of Radio Wales to me, was vehement in his opposition. On this issue, there was no meeting of minds. With the might of fellow journalists lining up behind him, he dug in his heels and I dug in mine.

Gareth was an experienced journalist with a long record of accomplishment in newspapers and radio. A Merthyr man – he did not speak Welsh – with a deep knowledge of South Wales communities, he was never afraid to voice his opinions and to fight, with characteristic stubbornness, those causes close to his heart. I was a populist. He was not. On more than one occasion, he told me that I was turning Radio Wales into a Radio Woolworths. He could be bolshie and difficult. He saw little merit in change, or in widening the appeal. He believed the rolling current affairs programme, Radio 4 type, should remain under the news department banner. I wanted news and analysis to become fixed points in a gentler topical sequence with music. Gareth thought it madness. I listened, but while respecting his opinion, I had to tell him, the editor has the last word. He could be gruff and petulant; rarely did the countenance underneath the grey beard show emotion or irritation other than a narrowing of the eyes and an impatient tug at the moustache. However, despite many fierce disagreements between us on the role of news, he was never cynical or patronising. My concept for Radio Wales had been agreed with the wholehearted backing from programme management, but delivering a new programme schedule on-air can be a perilous undertaking. It requires a single-minded, at times even bloody-minded, attitude, and confidence, but above all, it requires enthusiastic belief, skills, and commitment from the team.

As the launch date drew near, I turned my attention to marketing the new service and its new frequency, 340 MHz Medium Wave. Someone in the press office devised the catchphrase 'Get On the Go with Three Four 0', a slogan which would have done justice to a new brand of laxative. We advertised, printed car stickers and beer mats, utilised all the usual marketing tools of the day, but by far the most effective was the use we made of community radio in the four-week period before 13 November 1978.

RTE, the Irish broadcasting organisation, had built a mobile, self-sufficient, radio station on wheels, which they used to promote the Gaelic language in rural communities. It included a studio, an operational area and a small transmitter with a broadcasting radius of between five and ten miles. We had carried out a similar experiment in Wales, to promote the morning Welsh-language service on a new FM wavelength and to entice listeners to buy FM radios. We adapted the concept to promote Radio Wales in the populated urban areas in South and North-East Wales, choosing the locations of Rhondda, Merthyr, Cwmbrân and Wrexham. The van was wheeled into a parking area, to remain for four days, allowing local people to make and broadcast their own programmes. All of it was designed to draw attention to the fact that Radio Wales intended to be a 'close to the people', inclusive service. The exercise, which we called *Radio Rhondda*, began in the De Winton public house car park on the main street in Tonypandy. This was an historic site, where troops sent by Winston Churchill attempted to quell rioting miners during the great strike of 1926.

I have never experienced such excitement, or witnessed such involvement, before or since. Everyone, from Blaen Rhondda at the top of the valley, to the bottom at Pontypridd, seemed to have a story to tell. They began communicating as in days of old and they discovered a deep sense of belonging and community. They could challenge their political leaders directly and they could pinpoint failures and successes in their local social and cultural services. The nondescript caravan took on the mantle of a palatial broadcasting house, as we filled every hour from six thirty in the morning to nine at night.

Radio Rhondda's impact was due, in the main, to the involvement of the local cable company. Reception in the narrow, steep, coal mining valleys had always been difficult, and Rediffusion Cable solved the problem by offering radio and television services free of interference. The majority of households took up the offer. Of the two radio channels, Radio 2 was by far the most popular. Subscriber figures for the Rhondda valleys pointed to a figure of 40,000 households. I persuaded the managing director of the company to replace Radio 2 with our four-day Rhondda community service, and its impact was extraordinary. We had a captive audience. Dewi Griffiths opened the microphone at six - thirty the first morning and invited anyone travelling to work down the valley, 'to hoot your horn'. During the next hour or so, buses, lorries, cars and motorbikes hooted their reply, a cacophony of sound filled the air, and many times that week I heard the comment, 'Its lovely to hear people like us on the radio'. They had been the forgotten people, too ordinary to have a real voice in the highbrow scheme of broadcasting in Wales.

The caravan moved, with a different team at the helm, to set up camp at Merthyr, Cwmbrân and Wrexham, and the reaction was similar to Rhondda. We certainly raised the public awareness of Radio Wales, but we had also raised the desire within those communities for a permanent radio station. Unfortunately, the Managing Director of Rediffusion, although sympathetic, did not feel he could do the same deal when Radio Wales began. The cost of it would have been an imposition on those subscribers who had already paid to hear Radio 2.

Although the official launch date was Monday, 13 November, I like to think the service really began to operate two days earlier, on Saturday, 11 November. It was all due to rugby and the long-awaited confrontation of Wales v New Zealand at the Arms Park, a rugby game of singular significance. Match coverage was assured but I believed we could capture the spirit of anticipation, the build-up and the social essence of Cardiff on a big International day, in a six-and-a-half hour programme sequence hosted by Cliff Morgan. These were the days of the winning seventies and there was swagger and pride on the sporting fields of Wales.

The social epicentre of the nation, as well as being the Welsh team headquarters, was the Angel Hotel, directly opposite the Arms Park. Resources were stretched to the limit. Aerials for radio microphones swung drunkenly on the end of a floor brush projecting from a side bedroom window of the hotel, our operational centre for the morning, where I tried to guide Cliff through the running order of interviews and music.

As the eight o'clock news ended, *Morning of the Match* began. Cliff walked slowly up a hushed Westgate Street, describing the anticipation of a city waiting for a gladiatorial contest. He talked to Bill Harding, the groundsman, and he walked without warning into the hotel dining room, where Clive Rowlands, the coach, and other team members were eating their breakfast. The lighthearted banter heralded a morning of humour, memories, stories and discussion, not only about past rugby encounters, but about our uniqueness as a people. Cliff was inspired with truly remarkable focus and warmth. He was only slightly thrown, when I shouted at him during an interview with a leading member of the judiciary, via the talkback earpiece, that the microphone sound was breaking up.

'Your aerial has become entwined around your *be chi'n galw* (what d'you call it) in your trousers. Stand up.'

He had experienced much worse on the rugby field during his playing days and, with a mere shake of his leg, he carried on. During the last hour or so before kick off, our bedroom operational area turned into a mini crowd scene set, as colleagues and interested listeners came to see 'where it was all happening'. Later, when I received the listener returns, I saw how the audience had grown significantly through the morning transmission.

Our programme ended as the action moved into the main arena. A deep silence descended on the hotel. Someone had left us champagne. Too exhausted to go to the game, we slumped into dining-room chairs, drained from the excitement of our labours. The programme was later nominated for a Sony award. Cliff continued to give unstinting support to Radio Wales, travelling once a fortnight to present a programme of his favourite music, in addition to his work as Head of Television Sport and Outside Broadcasts. *Sounds Unforgettable* he called it, and it attracted huge audiences at lunchtime on Sundays. I shall always be grateful to him for his dedication and friendship.

There was little time to linger and savour. We had begun the countdown to Monday and I had a zillion-long checklist. We had found time to make a few trial runs of programmes and sequences but it was not enough. I was confident of the concept for the channel – a mixture of speech and music – but I was concerned about whether a young, inexperienced staff would deliver programmes with skill and authority. There was also the continued schism and bickering from news journalists, who believed the new schedule to be a diminution of their role and output at peak broadcasting hours – morning, lunchtime, and late afternoon. My request to them was to look at other ways of producing shorter, brighter, well-written, hard news programmes. They simply could not, or would not, take on board the concept that we were moving away from the Radio 4 style. New teams were in place to produce new programmes.

On Monday, the early morning programme, *A.M.*, presented by Anita Morgan, began promptly at 6.30 and I could almost feel in the air the resentment of many regular listeners when the first record of light music was played. This was an affront, a dumbing downwards rollercoaster, they said. In their eyes and ears, it was a monumental mistake. The buffeting reached a crescendo during the week. The journalists smiled in righteous satisfaction, but evidence proved that we were reaching out to new listeners. A phone-in programme a week later showed a fifty-fifty reaction to the new channel, and there was a slight increase in favour when our first official audience figures were released.

However, that did not stop the protesters. Middle Wales, like Middle England, was alive and well, and I received very many letters of abuse and criticism. Madeleine, my PA, carried a large bundle into my office one morning. Loyal to the end, but never one to mince words, she said, 'If I were you, I'd be worried.'

At their first meeting since the launch, The Broadcasting Council in Wales reported that they were not pleased with the early morning sequence but that there were many good programmes.

I did not dismiss criticisms; there was much to consider and there was a great deal of editorial analysis and change during the next months. My team remained steadfast and hard working, but the dissident, paranoid journalists had found allies. As men possessed, they set about the policy, regularly leaking titbits of gossip to the press, and writing directly about the 'travesty of radio in Wales' to the Director General. It was a baptism of boiling oil and I know I would never have coped without the sustained backing and encouragement of my superiors: Geraint Stanley Jones, the Head of Programmes, and his Deputy, Gareth Price. The lesson I learned from Lorraine all those years ago on how to handle criticism and praise also proved invaluable, together with the experience of having to deal with a similar onslaught, when the Welsh-language early-morning sequence of speech and music, *Helo Bobol,* first went on air in 1973.

There were faults, many of them, but I had given myself between four and six months to analyse and assess. I remained convinced, however, that the new concept worked, but we needed to execute a few programmes in the schedule with greater skill, appeal and authority. I tackled news division head-on, and slowly, Gareth Bowen and I reached a point where we could discuss matters amicably and with respect for each other. A few programmes changed, we dropped others, but the main casualty was Anita Morgan. She was and is a superb communicator and a sensitive programme-maker, but her appeal and style were not suitable for the early morning. She had been the target of a great deal of vicious criticism. Dismissing anyone is painful. I kept the decision to myself for days, rehearsing the reasons and arguments repeatedly in my mind. There were to be no leaks or letters before she heard the news. I was determined to tell her face to face. She would be bruised, but I was keen, if possible in such circumstances, to preserve her dignity and her pride. We met at my home, not in the office. I told her quietly; it took only a few minutes and her reaction to being dismissed after only six months was one of real anger and keen disappointment.

'Who is going to take over?' she asked.

I replied, 'Chris Stuart.'

Anita got up from her chair, and left, making only one comment: 'He's not Welsh!'

The following morning, she telephoned to say that she was naturally disappointed at my decision. She didn't agree, but she accepted it. Unlike a few others I dealt with in later years, Anita coped with her public hurt without conceit, pompous indignation or vanity, and she went on to make memorable documentary and feature programmes.

Five

It had been an exhausting first year, but the gains for Radio Wales were a real pleasure. Young producers, following their baptism of fire, were rapidly gaining confidence in their skills, and developing the necessary perspective to make good programmes. Chris Stuart brought stability to the early morning strand with his laid-back, easy microphone manner, sharp mind and a journalistic understanding. Listeners trusted him and enjoyed his company. He was multi-talented, a musician and a writer of songs and revues, who had trained in journalism after graduating. The fact that he was not Welsh and his accent had a hint of Brummie vowels and intonation, mattered little. Every morning he presented an instinctive grasp of Wales and its people.

Experienced broadcasters of the calibre of Alun Williams, Vincent Kane, Cliff Morgan, Maureen Staffer and Mari Griffith played a major role in the schedule of programmes and were steadfastly supportive, as was G. V. Wynne Jones, known everywhere as Geevers, the great rugby commentator. It was a joy to persuade him back to the microphone following years in the wilderness because of an altercation with the Union. It seemed outrageous that his gifts as a broadcaster had been sidelined, and he was delighted, 'in old age,' to present a regular half-hour programme of highlights and comment on the week's programmes.

We encouraged new talent and voices too. We advertised on

air for presenters, and over a thousand applied. I sifted through applications and tapes, a process that took weeks, before I eventually whittled them down to thirty possibles for audition, but there was one applicant who scored for originality and persistence. In the post every morning, there would be a card containing whimsical drawings and sketches of humorous thoughts and observations on topics of the day. Madeleine made sure that the author was auditioned. 'You've got see him. He may be mad, but he's funny and different. He's from Aberdare.'

It was Roy Noble, allowing his imagination to run riot from the cares of his work as a respected junior school headmaster in Powys. He began broadcasting by giving short talks, which he called *Letter from Aberdare*. Later, we encouraged him to think of making radio his full-time career. It took time and many discussions. It was a difficult decision, to give up teaching and secure employment for the whims and insecurities of broadcasting. I offered him a two-year contract to present a daily radio programme and, twenty years on, he has won awards and accolades and has carved a unique relationship with listeners. He epitomises the 'close to the people' concept of the early days. Above it all, he invites Wales to smile in the mornings.

The mix of voices and accents from different areas of Wales was important to the service; so was a love of words and language. Too often, aspiring young presenters who came to auditions did so believing that the transatlantic American accent, encouraged by commercial radio stations, was the appropriate presentation mode for all broadcasters. Frank Hennessy was a distinctive voice at CBC, the Cardiff commercial radio station, his accent and dialect unique to the city. He was also a writer of folk songs and a member of the folk group, The Hennessys. He joined us in order to extend his radio presentation work, and his wry, homely style soon endeared him to listeners, as did the individual humour of Owen Money from Merthyr Tydfil.

Emphasis was placed on political matters during that first winter of Radio Wales, the last of the seventies. It was the winter of discontent, with serious unrest and strikes in the public-service sector – uncollected rubbish littered the streets, bodies waiting for burial were stacked up in funeral homes, and ambulance services were seriously disrupted. Against that background, voting on the issue of devolution was planned to take place on 1 March 1979, and we were obliged to cover the democratic process in some detail, providing a platform for debate and discussion on the Labour Government's proposals. There was a belief that many of the non-Welsh-speaking members of staff were biased against a Welsh assembly, and Welsh speakers biased in favour. That was not true, but there was a degree of antagonism and hostility against the language, as I had found on taking up the editorship of Radio Wales. Often, the coverage of meetings held by movements hostile to the language received far too much attention in topical news programmes.

However, the campaign for devolution was not dynamic; it failed to stimulate much interest, although there were regular reports, phone-ins and confrontational exchanges in our programme schedule. 'Devolution is a waste of money and unnecessary,' was the comment most often heard from those interested enough to voice an opinion. The turnout was low, and when the referendum result was announced, only thirty-three per cent had voted in favour of devolution and a Welsh Assembly.

It was almost twenty years later before Wales had the confidence to produce a positive 'Yes' vote and for an assembly to become a reality.

Within two months, with the General Election due in May, we were in the throes of another political battle. Radio Wales set up its own daily coverage of the campaign, and, on voting day, we broadcast our own assessment and independent results service. The Conservatives swept into power, with Mrs Thatcher at the helm – the first woman Prime Minister in history – and her policies for the economy, the unions, and broadcasting were to have far-reaching repercussions on Welsh society for years.

Before the full effect of political change manifested itself, Radio Cymru became a full, national service in 1979. Meirion Edwards was appointed its first Editor, the same day as I was made Editor Radio Wales, and although he was able to expand his output during the autumn and winter of 1978, it took twelve months before officialdom and finance gave the service its blessing. Meirion and I worked together harmoniously but we were in competition for listeners, for those who spoke Welsh also spoke English. Meirion had begun his broadcasting career as a radio talks producer in the sixties. He had left the BBC to take up a post as lecturer in Drama at the University of Wales, Bangor, before returning to broadcasting as Head of Production in Bangor. There had been a long history and tradition of making a range of Welsh-language radio programmes from the beginnings of the Welsh Home Service. Radio programmes in English had tended to be confined to news and current affairs, until the extension of hours for the *Nine Five* series. A few documentaries, music and orchestral programmes and drama productions made specifically in Wales for network radio supplemented it. These were high-cost programmes broadcast mainly on Radios 4 and 3.

My job, in addition to looking after the Radio Wales output, was to generate more programme-making for the networks and to liaise closely with London production departments. We were a year or so into the next decade before the young production staff could be truly effective and confident when they sold their ideas. The first was a moving documentary by Kate Fenton on the effect on a family in Caerphilly of a violent attack on their daughter by a man with an axe. The production won praise for its clarity and sensitivity. Radio Cymru's producers chose not to put additional pressure on themselves, preferring to concentrate solely on programme-making for their own service. I always felt that the network dimension, reflecting life in all its facets to a wider audience, improved production skills and gave our service greater confidence and coherence.

Although there was a competitive edge to our relationship, Meirion and I worked closely towards the goal of improving radio in Wales. We eked out our financial programme budgets and often arranged to share limited resources. Never was this more apparent than in our sports programme reports, commentaries and results on Saturday afternoons. Sport was an important aspect of our weekend schedule and had a substantial following.

The producer Thomas Davies – experienced, disciplined and focused – simultaneously and almost single-handedly produced two sports programmes, in two languages. Luckily, his team included experienced presenters, reporters and commentators for live rugby and soccer games, but organising the logistics for the twin operation was extremely complex. Studio 6 on Saturdays was the control centre, and Tom, headphones on his head, issued his commands with skilled precision, alternating commentaries and reports in Welsh and English from grounds all over Wales. Followers of sport are demanding; reports and results must be accurate and on time, and Tom rarely failed his listeners. When transmission ended at around six-thirty, he went home to listen to recordings of both programmes. On Monday morning, in his review to staff, he noted lapses of concentration, reported inaccuracies and any misuse of language, in Welsh or English. He demanded high standards and total commitment from everyone.

Peter Walker, his presenter, the former Glamorgan cricketer and an accomplished broadcaster, earned his living as a freelance and spread his talents among as many radio and TV outlets as possible. He reserved Saturday for Radio Wales sport, but Tom did not regard this as adequate preparation and pre-recording time for a complex, live, six-hour sports programme. Tom asked for more time, especially on the Friday before transmission. Peter argued that time was money and he had his living to consider. He had never failed the programme and Tom had his undivided attention on Saturdays. They failed to resolve their differences, it became acrimonious, and Peter was asked to stand down. On this issue, I supported Tom. He was not a hard man but he was deeply committed to his programme and he required the same attitude from his team.

Such dedication was to be treasured but not exploited, and when the BBC Board of Governors held one of their monthly meetings in Cardiff, we were able to put our concerns to its members and to the management team. It was not a meeting of minds, and it was not a level playing field, but it was an opportunity to voice opinions and to lobby. I should have known better. Outside Wales, they lobby. Inside Wales, so I have been informed by those who live outside, we whinge.

During lunch, somewhere around trifle time, Meirion and I asked the Director General, Ian Trethowan, why the centre found it so difficult to appreciate that we operated two national radio services, not one. If we were to achieve quality and standard, we needed adequate finance. Scotland employed thirty-seven producers to produce one service. We ran two services with seventeen producers. A glazed look settled on his face. It bubbled into anger. He leant forward, lifted his pudding spoon to emphasise his words, his voice thin and mean, bursting into staccato sentences. 'Scotland has twice the population of Wales. The overall radio budget is carved equally between the National Regions: Wales, Scotland and Northern Ireland. It is up to Wales's management to divide and manage its slice of the cake.' We pursued the argument to little avail. The devolution campaign was over and lost. The pressure had evaporated.

Radio Wales faced calmer waters in the approaching decade, but the last year of the seventies had been turbulent. The service was inclusive, the schedule had been strengthened, and I hoped our programme mix had increased an awareness of the Welsh identity. The experience, on occasions, had been lonely and difficult. There were also periods of self-doubt, but radio is a people business and there were many on whom I came to rely for support and honest appraisal.

I had always been fortunate in my secretaries and PAs. They all became good friends. Elvira Davies and Megan Evans, both Cardiganshire ladies, were sympathetic and hard working.

Madeleine joined me two years before Radio Wales was launched, and we had worked together on many programmes in the *Nine Five* series, the Wynford Vaughan Thomas walk, and, later, she experienced her first National Eisteddfod. She witnessed and helped my progress from producer to editor to manager. Soon, she became a friend and confidant and has remained so over the years, but occasionally, when my irritations surfaced, the going got rough and I became too demanding, she would remind me, 'I only applied for the job because no-one else wanted to work with you.'

She had returned to work when her children, Sally and Simon, were in high school. Tall, dark haired, stylish and smart, with a confident, straightforward manner, her office, where she often held court at the end of the day, would be alive with the sound of inconsequential gossip and laughter. If she disagreed with one of my decisions, she voiced her views in a no-nonsense manner, and, on more than one occasion, she stopped me in my tracks to make me reconsider. Many colleagues misunderstood the kind of banter and friendship between us as inappropriate between boss and secretary, but at work, there was a line we did not cross. Trust and loyalty work both ways. When my marriage disintegrated and I left home, a few days before the launch of Radio Wales, and my new flat was not ready, Madeleine and her family took me in and looked after me.

In 1985, tragedy struck her life. Her husband, Steve, was killed in a car crash. Six months later, an 'over the limit' car driver killed her daughter, Sally, within days of her wedding, as she stepped out of a taxi outside her home. Madeleine coped then and still does. The scars remain but the spirit and the banter, which for a while was obliterated by the pain of loss, has returned.

I have often been asked whether I was right to attempt such a monumental change of style and approach on Radio Wales listeners. My answer is always yes, and I have few regrets on that score. I may have attempted too much too soon, making too many editorial errors in the first few months. In this business, precocious talent and boundless enthusiasm do not always compensate for a lack of production experience. Too often, producers lacked the cutting edge, the knowledge and the 'nose' to put a stamp of authority on the output. We made our mistakes but there was an equal number of benefits, and I guess that my greatest pleasure came from the realisation that we had changed the audience profile and we had extended the reach. Radio in Wales developed an identity, it became more inclusive, and a growing number of listeners gave it a stamp of approval. On reflection, I suppose if I got another chance, in another life, I would get it right first time.

Megan Stuart who became Editor Radio Wales

Two good friends, brothers and singers Andrew and Dennis O'Neill.

And two close colleagues, Gareth Price and Gwilym Owen in convivial mood.

(Above) Celebrating with Iwan Thomas (left) during the tribute dinner at the City Hall, Cardiff in honour of the comedian, Wyn Calvin.

Television is a serious business! John Stuart Roberts, Head of Television (left) and John Watkin, Head of Press and Public Relations.

The team photograph of the visit to India in 1984 to film Prime Minister Indira Gandhi. From left to right: Tom Friswell, cameraman; Shyam Verma; Teleri Bevan; Mrs Indira Gandhi;

Brenda Thomas, PA; John Welsh, lighting; John Watkin, producer; Jeff North, sound; and Ashley Cole, assistant cameraman.

At the Taj Mahal shrine with Shyam Verma.

Setting up to interview Benazir Bhutto at her country home in Larnaca during her first election campaign.

Madeleine and John Hefin taking time out at Lake Louise during the Banff Film Festival.

The Eighties

One

Mrs Thatcher was into her first year as Prime Minister when 1980 dawned, and her policies for the economy, the unions and broadcasting were beginning to take effect. She believed, as did many members of her government, that the BBC was profligate and wasteful, and controlling the licence fee was the only method of putting 'real pressure' for reform on the organisation. She did so by keeping the licence at the same level for the next five years, at a time when ITV's revenue from advertising was at an all-time high. It gave commercial companies the opportunity to plan for expansion, especially during daytime. Breakfast television dawned, with TV-AM promising a lively beginning to every day, but the BBC, its long tradition of being the pioneering leader in broadcasting now being questioned, decided to launch its own breakfast TV programme a fortnight earlier than ITV and at half the cost.

That decision was the first of many changes to the structure of broadcasting. The speed of technological advances, the development of cable and satellite systems, and the increasing use of video machines, tapes and recordings had major cost implications for broadcasters. So began the drive for economy and efficiency. We had entered the era of controlled financial budgeting and a completely new way of housekeeping. We tightened our belts, we sliced our cakes thinly and we turned our screws tightly. We were instructed to be responsible and accountable for the total cost of our programmes; the decade of free enterprise and market forces was upon us, and accountants and financiers were coming to grips with programme-making and the ephemeral nature of broadcasting. The days of artistic risk-taking seemed numbered. Cost effectiveness and giving value for money were the top requirements, and increasingly, broadcasting was now to be regarded as a business and an industry.

Producers and editors had to change their working practices. No longer could we rely on planners and dark-suited gentlemen with their arcane powers to allocate resources, to plan our schedules and to assist with financial budgeting. The emphasis changed. Departments and individual producers took on added responsibilities, with a new set of criteria and controls for every aspect of programme-making. They became more akin to administrators, and production departments began hiring teams of financial assistants to deal with complex television productions.

The radio operation was simpler and more flexible, with budgets and costs per hour much smaller. We could react swiftly to change. For instance, when government proposals began to have an impact on industry and manufacturing, one of the first casualties in Wales came with the closure of the large Shotton steelworks on Deeside, in North East Wales. Hundreds of workers were made redundant and a close-knit community was left shocked and devastated.

Exercising the right of greater autonomy in Wales, Geraint Stanley Jones, the Head of Programmes responsible for radio and television, determined that BBC Wales should set up a community radio station in Shotton, to act as an information centre and a counselling service. Gareth Bowen headed the small team and, for sixteen weeks, the service they provided received widespread praise from people of the area and from politicians and local-government officials. It met an immediate social need; the station acted as a catalyst to a community that in the past had felt neglected by BBC Wales. The North/South divide had tended to become more apparent as resources for Radio Wales were centred in Cardiff.

Discussions and negotiations between broadcasters and local government leaders continued long after Radio Deeside had closed, so that by the autumn of 1981 a more permanent solution had been found. With financial assistance from the local authority, Radio Clwyd was established, serving a much larger area, which included the towns of Mold and Wrexham. It began as a news service at peak listening times of the day, morning, lunchtime and late afternoon. It was effective, and local enthusiasm for the station soon forced it to increase its time on air, to provide entertainment and information for much of every morning. The two staff journalists produced news programmes, but local volunteers presented all other general interest programmes. Two years later, another community station, Radio Gwent, was established to serve the populated South East corner of Wales. Both stations underlined the identity of Radio Wales, but further fragmentation by increasing the number of community stations for other areas was firmly rejected. Such a policy would have meant Radio Wales losing its coherence as a radio service, because each community station would exercise the right to opt out of the national service to broadcast its own material.

Commercial radio companies took up the challenge and franchises were offered to other local communities. Following Swansea Sound came CBC, in Cardiff, in 1980, and Marcher Sound, based in Wrexham, served the North East. The battle for audiences was truly upon us. I was attempting to strengthen the Radio Wales schedule, enriching the mix of programmes. Enid Williams increased our drama productions for network, and Kate Fenton, a talented researcher, made documentaries on a regular basis. A new arts series began, with journalist Adam Hopkins in the chair. Richard Thomas, at the time a producer with the *Meet For Lunch* team, was beginning to show promise as a writer. His surreal comedy series, *Auntie Nellie's Handbag*, with Sion Probert and Myfanwy Talog, won universal praise, but our enthusiasm for such innovation and risk was soon tempered when we were told to cut the schedule by five hours a week. Daytime broadcasting hours, the heart of the schedule, remained untouched and most of the cuts came from high-cost evening programmes.

The first two years of leading Radio Wales had given me grounding in the skills of management. Initially, I had concentrated on editorial matters – developing ideas and scheduling programmes – but the change of emphasis in financial accountability gave me much more control of my programme budgets and total resource costing. I welcomed this responsibility. The editor was turning into a manager, and despite the hierarchical structure of the BBC, with its long line of managerial reference points, the programme heads in Wales allowed me the freedom to administrate and operate my radio service.

Geraint Stanley Jones was a firm and encouraging Head of Programmes. He had vigorously defended the changes and policies of Radio Wales when the criticism was at its fiercest. He was not a garrulous person, nor was he a leader always seeking the limelight. He was a contemplative and conceptual thinker, occasionally emotional, at his best discussing ideas with individual producers.

167

When he first took charge of programmes, there was tentativeness, an apparent lack of decisiveness about him. He was a people person, never afraid to take risks, who grew into the job. Those of us who worked closely with him soon realised the strength of his views and saw how effective he could be at defending the public-service ethos. Quietly spoken, rarely raising his voice, listening seemingly impassively to other people's views, the contrast between the private and the public persona was never more apparent than when he relaxed at the piano, or the organ, to sing old-time ballads, or hymns of praise. At heart, he was a showman with a passion for music and entertainment, and when St. David's Hall, the splendid new concert hall in the centre of Cardiff, opened in the early eighties, Geraint saw the opportunity for the BBC Welsh Symphony Orchestra to make St. David's Hall its home for broadcast concerts.

The partnership between him and his deputy, Gareth, was effective because they complemented each other through their similarities and their differences. They were both large, tall, bearded men with a liking for the good things in life. Gareth was the organiser and the skilled negotiator. He tested other people's views against his own, systematically questioning opposing views every step of the way with patience and persistence. Rarely were there outbursts of irritability or temper, but there was unqualified firmness when he pushed through new policies and ideas. His great love of rugby was always apparent when he conducted negotiations for radio and television rights with the Welsh Rugby Union, and as home International match days approached, Gareth became the most popular man in BBC Wales. He took on the role of head of tickets. They were the WRU's allocation to the BBC for

International match days, and they were prized beyond measure. Gareth's battalion of close friends multiplied, and as kick-off time ticked nearer, the circle of men around him at our pre-match reception grew ever larger as he practised a sleight of hand, his lips barely moving behind the ginger beard, and the favoured few received their tickets. He was convivial, he revelled in the company of friends he trusted and with whom he could relax, gossip and argue.

Geraint and Gareth worked closely together for well on fifteen years; in some respects, this was too long a time, but in the mid-seventies, as a two-man programme directorate, they brought stability, and many of their achievements were notable and memorable: commissioning drama series such as Elaine Morgan's *Life and Times of Lloyd George,* promoting the Max Boyce entertainment shows for BBC 1, gentle nostalgic music programmes from Stuart Burrows, and the riotous interpretation of a rugby outing to Paris in *Grand Slam.*

In 1981, I became an administrator. Owen Edwards, who had been Controller BBC Wales for seven years, was appointed to head the new Welsh-language television channel, S4C. This caused an obvious managerial change at the top. Geraint Stanley Jones became Controller and Gareth Price was appointed Head of Programmes. It was a tried-and-tested team, which knew the BBC's system inside out. The only post in that hierarchical trinity to be advertised was that of Deputy Head of Programmes. I decided to put my head on the block and apply. This was a risk, because although I had some experience of television, I was very much a radio person, and the role of deputy carried responsibilities for television in addition to radio programmes. Television was complex, expensive and demanding and I lacked the inside practitioner's knowledge of new technology. Nevertheless, Radio Wales had given me experience in management, financial accounting and editorial skills. It was a risk, too, because I was 50. In an industry known to be a young man's game, I was a woman and ten years older than Gareth. On the plus side, I had experience and stamina and I had grown a few more skins as a result of my dealings with difficult, occasionally bolshie, individuals. It was likely I would meet a few more of them if I were to be successful in getting this job.

I came face to face with one of these people sooner than I expected, when my name appeared on the short list for interview. He was a respected and creative producer, who came to my office one late afternoon, to say bluntly, 'You should withdraw your candidacy. You shouldn't go through with the interview.' It astounded me. In order to enforce his views, he went on, 'There are others who feel like me.'

I had long realised that the close-knit, television, departmental collegiate system was fertile ground for nurturing bastards but this one headed the dirty tricks brigade. He outlined my weaknesses, as he perceived them, with stunning candour. He listed the difficulties I might face, adding that I should leave the field open to strong candidates from television. In fairness, he never once mentioned the fact that I was a woman applying for a senior job, but it was a brutal display of undermining pressure. Of course, it had the opposite effect. It strengthened my resolve. My face may have betrayed the odd emotional twitch, a certain redness might have stained my cheeks, but I remained cool, an equal; I knew then that if I were successful, the knives would be drawn. He left the office, no doubt pleased in his own mind that I would do his bidding. I did not. Neither did I hint at the effect his words had had on me. I knew there were three candidates, all from television production, and I finished our ill-judged meeting by quoting a well-known boardroom platitude, 'It is open competition. The Board will decide.'

It had been a wonderful illustration of the claustrophobic atmosphere within television departments, in which scheming and plotting by a few Machiavellian individuals was becoming a way of life. The majority of programme people, as I found them, were much too independent-minded and inventive to join conspiracies.

I duly went for the interview and I remember it for two reasons. I was treated as an equal. No-one dared ask how I would cope 'as a woman'. The Equal Pay and Sex Discrimination Acts, together with the active Equal Opportunities Commission, were becoming effective. More surprising was the final question they put to me, 'How do you define Welshness?'

I muttered something like, 'Have you got an hour?'

There was laughter but it was a question relevant to the time. It meant attempting to interpret the signposts which defined our national identity; it covered matters such as the influences of history and language, devolution, winning rugby matches, our industrial history, oppression, culture, male voice choirs, Welsh National Opera, and, of course, religion. It encompassed these matters and very many more. I was thankful when the interview concluded. I left the building to take an extended lunch and to review the experience with Madeleine. At the end of the day, I heard that I had been successful. The job was mine. I was to begin almost immediately. I moved into an even larger office, on the third floor, with a huge desk in one corner. I also inherited a larger fridge from

Gareth Price. Offices in a hierarchical organisation were a symbol of status. The managerial enclave at Broadcasting House was 'The third floor', and attempting to operate an open-door policy in which members of staff could be encouraged to 'call any time' was difficult. The corridor, sombre and dark, opulently wood panelled, had a reputation for being intimidating; the monastic silence implied an atmosphere of contemplation, even a place for meaningful decision-taking. Those brave enough to ask, 'Have you got a minute?' often received short shrift from protective PAs. One producer became so irritated by the stalling that he went to the fourth floor, to drop a placard from a window directly outside the Head of Programmes office window. It carried the plea, 'Can I see you, please?'

I was sad to leave Radio Wales; the difficulties of the past three years had been made pleasurable by watching the young and energetic production people ripen into proficient programme-makers. The service had matured and had gained authority. A new man, Robert Atkins, took over the editorship. He was a producer in the World Service and had been invited by the London radio directorate to assess and report on the national services in Scotland, Ulster and Wales. He was ambitious, extremely knowledgeable on broadcasting, but not an instinctive practitioner. I had the distinct feeling that coming to Wales was a calculated career move that was meant to be a stepping-stone to greater things. As it turned out, Bob left for academia, making his home in Wales, lecturing at the School of Journalism.

Excitement and nervous apprehension accompanied me to the brave new world on the third floor. The structure of television in Wales was about to change forever with the setting up of S4C, and I was involved again in shaping a new channel. The role of

Deputy was a strange position, never clearly defined. The deputy can influence, but I also realised the danger of being a mere managerial clearinghouse, running the administrative bits-and-pieces such as checking and signing expenses forms. Gareth and I understood each other and soon we were able to work out a fruitful working partnership, although I felt at times that I could have turned out to be a 'maid of all work'. The two editors managed and ran the two radio services, but television production was divided into departments: drama, light entertainment, sport, religion, documentaries, news and current affairs, and children. The heads of those departments had direct access to the head of programmes and were seen individually, on a regular basis, to discuss new ideas and on-going editorial matters. The system worked and communication was always open and fruitful.

In the early eighties, as the effect of the new buzz words, accountability and responsibility, took effect, the BBC held management courses and I was ordered to attend a two-week course in a large Victorian pile in deepest Buckinghamshire.

Twenty-nine men and I gathered in a spacious conference room, on a Monday morning in October; such was the gender distribution in management personnel at the time in the BBC. My designated place was at the top of one arm of the horseshoe-shaped table, close to the rostrum. Without exception, every speaker who came to talk to us began pointedly, 'Lady and gentlemen'. On the course were high-ranking engineers, planners, organisers, editors, administrators and a sprinkling of chief assistants. They were the nomads of the BBC, either singled out to gain experience for promotion, or worn-out misfits, or those who had been sent upstairs to prop up ineffective managers.

During the fortnight, we had lectures on managerial theories, especially financial, by captains of industry, directors of large public and private institutions and members of the BBC's board of management. During the afternoons, we divided into groups, to discuss problems and to suggest solutions to some of the pressing issues facing the broadcasting industry. We spent much of the time looking deep into the corporate crystal ball, and discussed the effect on the BBC of the first of many satellite channels, and the competition faced by BBC 2 from the new Channel 4. I don't recall many dynamic solutions, it was a rather gentle kind of course, although there were some hard-fought croquet matches on the great lawn. The final lecture, on the last Friday, was given by the BBC staff doctor, who gave a real pointer to the future of pressure and deadlines. His countenance in permanent lament, he urged us, whatever our workload, to maintain a healthy lifestyle, and warned us to be vigilant and to look for the first signs of stress in our staff. I paid my bar bill for the fortnight and left.

Two

The story of how the Welsh-language television channel, S4C, was established is historic and was, at times, dramatic. It followed twenty years of campaigning, led in the last ten by the vocal and disruptive actions of Cymdeithas yr Iaith Gymraeg. The all-pervading influence of television was believed to be accelerating the decline in the number of Welsh speakers, but not everyone agreed that all Welsh-language television programmes should be placed on the one channel. Many feared such a concept would create a television ghetto for a minority language unable to compete effectively for viewers against the might of the popular TV channels. Their preferred solution was to maintain the status quo, continuing the practice of scheduling Welsh-language programmes as opt-outs from BBC 1. Any increase in the number of Welsh programmes would mean displacing even more programmes from the popular channel. This was a nightmare proposal for broadcasters. For years, they had suffered angry protestations from those who had no choice but to watch, at peak times, programmes in a language they didn't understand. A separate channel was the only solution. Committees and enquiries, their names have a particular ring about them – Crawford, Pilkington, Siberry and Annan – had all, in their turn, attempted to solve the problem. The possibility of a clear-cut decision came to a head when the fourth television channel became available.

The new Conservative Government, in its manifesto before the 1979 election, had recognised the need for a Welsh television channel. Hopes were high that the new Broadcasting Bill, when it was announced, would include provision for the Welsh language on the fourth channel. Six months later, those hopes were dashed, when the Home Secretary, William Whitelaw, declared that, having considered all the options, he had decided, after all, that Welsh-language television programmes should remain on BBC and ITV.

There was a furious reaction to the announcement. Broadcasters declared the scheme unworkable, calling the proposal 'fatally flawed'; viewers in Wales believed it would intensify the linguistic divisions within communities. Language activists escalated their campaign of civil disruption. In the spring of 1980 came a dramatic announcement from Gwynfor Evans, President of Plaid Cymru, who declared he intended fasting to death unless the government reversed its decision. The fast would begin in October. No-one doubted his determination. A man of deep conviction, an ardent pacifist and a strong leader of Welsh nationalism, he demanded that the fourth channel in Wales should be a Welsh-language channel, and that it should receive adequate funding. That summer was one of intense political activity. It culminated in a deputation meeting the Home Secretary. The former Secretary of State for Wales, Cledwyn Hughes; high-ranking civil servant, Sir Goronwy Daniel; and the Archbishop of Wales, the Rev. G. O. Williams, led it. Their main concern was that, unless the government reconsidered its decision, civil unrest in Wales would become a reality. A few weeks later, in the autumn of 1980, William Whitelaw changed his mind again. He had bowed to pressure. He proposed that, in Wales, a separate and independent Welsh Fourth Channel Authority would be established, with a board to administer and regulate its activities. Gwynfor Evans, when he had satisfied himself of the funding arrangements – a levy on the revenues of ITV – accepted the scheme and called off his fast before the October deadline.

The broadcasters, BBC and HTV, as the main suppliers of Welsh programmes for the new channel, had much to consider. The fourth channel was a new and different concept. Programmes from both organisations would be scheduled side by side on the same channel. There would also be a third supplier. For the first time, television would involve producers from the independent sector. Differences of approach and style between the three suppliers was a matter of concern, and for the BBC, the public service body funded by the licence fee, the difference caused unease. Over the years, the BBC had developed an 'in house' style; programmes were produced by teams of people with a range of skills, according to its editorial needs. It scheduled them and it transmitted them. The new fourth channel was not to be a producer of programmes; it was a broadcaster, or a publisher. It was commercially funded and would show advertisements. All these factors came into play when we, in the BBC, came to discuss scheduling and the commissioning of programmes. The relationship between the various bodies contributing to the channel's operation was to be critical to its development in the early months.

I joined Gareth Price as his deputy, to begin planning the BBC's role and contribution. Owen Edwards had left and was already installed as Chief Executive of the new channel, which had now taken the name S4C (*Sianel 4 Cymru* – Channel 4 Wales). The government had stipulated that the BBC should produce a minimum of ten hours of programmes per week, and had indicated that, when the next licence-fee negotiations took place, funding would be ring-fenced for the extra programme output. The ten hours made by the BBC and paid for by the licence fee would be free for the new Authority to schedule. However, finance became a contentious issue between BBC Wales and London and remained so during the eighties. The argument raged that it was folly for the BBC to divert twelve million pounds for a channel with a potential audience of 500,000 Welsh-speaking viewers, when the main BBC networks, the popular television channels, faced cuts because the licence fee had not been increased. However, a deadline had been set; S4C would be launched on 1 November 1982. Time was short.

The first problem for us at the planning stage was the question of scheduling and editorial control; sensitive issues because of our history as a producer, scheduler and broadcaster. It seemed, at first, that we in the BBC were in danger of acting as a mere facilities house, making programmes at the bidding of another Authority. It was a concept we strongly resisted. The licence fee funded our programmes; they were not to be paid for by S4C. It was necessary, therefore, to safeguard their identity within the schedule, and not to show them surrounded by advertisements. One idea proposed that BBC programmes should be transmitted as one block in the nightly schedule. It was dismissed immediately as unworkable. A scheduler places programme sequences on a particular night, in a particular order, and at a particular time, in order to maximise their effectiveness and appeal to viewers. We were programme people, and an agreement was eventually reached, whereby no advertisements would be shown at the beginning or end of BBC programmes. Nevertheless, the most difficult issue was that of editorial control. It was our right to decide what programmes we produced and to maintain control on the production process, and producers were not to believe they were working for another authority. These principles and agreements seem today, twenty years on, to be draconian, but as we planned and discussed, there came an understanding and a measure of give and take between two sides.

Recruitment for the expansion came next. We were increasing our Welsh-language output from seven to ten hours a week; not a huge increase, but the range and mix of our productions would widen. It gave us the opportunity to make light-entertainment programmes on a regular basis, to widen the scope of our drama and documentary departments and to enrich the channel's schedule with orchestral and other music programmes. At the end of the recruitment process, we had expanded by 300 personnel, making BBC Wales the largest broadcasting centre outside London. There was not enough room to house all television departments at Broadcasting House, and the search for suitable premises began in earnest. Eventually an unprepossessing, post-war, brick building was found, standing in acres of green fields, a mile and a half from Llandaff. It had been the headquarters of British Steel in South Wales, and its spacious office accommodation and wide corridors were symbolic of the growth and importance of steel production to the economy of Wales in the twentieth century. The sale of the Gabalfa building to the BBC in 1981 was a sign that the steel industry was in terminal decline, and that the Thatcher government's policies for public sector industries were taking effect.

Gabalfa was by no means an ideal location, because of the distance between the building and Broadcasting House. We were not, as an establishment, housed under one roof, and television producers were obliged to travel between their offices and their technical resources: studios, video editing, graphics and all engineering departments. There grew a 'them and us' culture. It was imperceptible but it was there, and it flourished. Producers wanted to be at the heart of things, to be part of the programme decision-making process, especially with a new channel coming into operation. It took another eight years for suitable accommodation to be found and bought; it was the former School of Home Economics, directly opposite Broadcasting House. It was renamed Tŷ Oldfield (Oldfield House) to mark the long tenure of Alun Oldfield Davies as Controller, BBC Wales.

As the logistics came together, we began making programmes. It had been agreed that BBC Wales would continue to provide news programmes for S4C, although this decision came in for some hard bargaining with HTV, the other main broadcaster involved. Almost since its inception in 1968, the commercial company had produced a topical news magazine called *Y Dydd* (The Day) shown as an opt-out from ITV. It was part of HTV's commitment to Welsh-language television, since it had won the franchise. The BBC, too, had produced a daily magazine programme called *Heddiw* (Today), broadcast as a regular opt-out from BBC 1. Both programmes, televised at different times in the early evening, were popular and commanded good audiences, despite the protestations from non-Welsh speakers. From 1 November, the situation was to change. S4C, if it was to attain authority as a channel, would require a strong news service, in addition to in-depth analysis and current affairs programmes. The initial agreement, based on the fact that the BBC could tap into the extensive London newsgathering operation, was a decisive factor. The ability to have available, in addition to news of Wales, national and international material on major stories of the day in the Welsh language was a first. It was a matter of editorial judgement how all the material was prioritised, interpreted, collated, edited and placed for a daily news programme, but it was vital to the authority of the service that its coverage should be comprehensive.

If BBC Wales was to provide a news service, HTV would concentrate on investigative current affairs programmes, an analysis of issues or 'the stories behind the stories'. On paper, the agreement seemed a satisfactory solution for both broadcasters, BBC and HTV. However, for our BBC journalists, working at the 'coalface', it was flawed. They found it frustrating and unsatisfactory to operate. They believed the news operation should have an additional programme outlet to analyse in depth and to investigate stories and issues. The demarcation line between the BBC's role and that of HTV was too rigid, they said. Journalists, by nature, are rarely content; their role is to question. The BBC editorial departmental structure, under the umbrella title News and Current Affairs, gave added strength to their aspirations as far as the S4C operation was concerned. This issue rumbled on for four years.

When agreement had been reached on most of the difficult planning issues, I was delegated to attend a fortnightly meeting with S4C programme managers, to discuss our future programme plans and scheduling. Their Head of Programmes, Euryn Ogwen Williams, and his planners conducted these meetings. We knew each other well. Euryn had taken part in a young people's panel game I presented during my TWW days, and, after graduating at the University of Wales, Bangor, he had blossomed as a television producer with HTV, before being appointed to fashion the new programme operation at S4C. He was a man of humour, charm and guile, a free spirit, a risk-taker, creative, and a poet, with all the attributes necessary to succeed as a negotiator and arbitrator, especially when he came face to face with prickly problems from the entrenched attitudes of other programme people. Euryn seemed to have avoided the protective coating of non-stick Teflon most young apprentice producers at HTV acquired. He was a shrewd operator, and his knowledge of the industry and his determination promised a channel of style and opportunity, and, immediately, he galvanised the independent sector. They were producers Euryn could commission directly, and without doubt, the most adventurous were those working in graphics and animation. Wales had no tradition in this field, but with encouragement and backing and limited time, six cartoons of Super Ted were produced by a small production house in time for the launch. They were acknowledged as a world-class product, attracting critical acclaim. Euryn had something different to sell and to market. He made the most of it.

The BBC by comparison seemed like a big juggernaut unable to sparkle with inventiveness. Seven of our ten hours were a mix of old programme favourites. They had been part of Welsh-language television for some time: *Pobol y Cwm* (People of the Valley), a popular weekly drama series, and *Dechrau Canu, Dechrau Canmol* (Hymns of Praise), together with news, and sport, featuring mainly coverage of rugby and snooker matches, religious discussions

182

and children's programmes. At our meetings in the early months, these programmes were often highlighted by one or two S4C apparatchiks as examples of the BBC's 'institutionalised attitude', lacking true creativity, risk and originality. I was accused of suffering from the malaise of BBC arrogance. I found smiling the best antidote in those circumstances. I would counter by drawing their attention to the audience figures; they attracted top ratings and appreciation. They were solid, well-produced, and underpinned the channel's schedule. Our output also included many new and different programmes such as a sparkling light-entertainment series, *Hapnod,* and a production of Gwenlyn Parry's powerful new controversial play, *Y Tŵr.* There was often that kind of pit-a-pat exchange and friction, but it was good gamesmanship, with Euryn sitting at the head of the table, quietly puffing on his pipe, smiling enigmatically, while he orchestrated the give and take.

Occasionally, friction turned to outbursts, and I remember Emlyn Davies, a forthright deputy to Euryn at S4C, declaring in a lecture he gave at the Celtic Film Festival held in Cardiff, that only independent producers gave value for money and made the most inventive and original programmes. Gareth and I, sitting in the audience, very nearly exploded. Gamesmanship had gone out of the window, especially when he cited the BBC's comfortable attitude towards the new channel. Had we publicly refuted the accusation, giving as evidence the harsh reality of the Corporation's contribution to the S4C schedule, it would have provided good copy for journalists and good sport for onlookers. Public coolness prevailed. Privately, many harsh words were exchanged.

Our right to retain editorial control remained a contentious issue on many occasions, especially during the first months. All the senior programme people at S4C had trained and gained experience of television with the BBC or HTV. Being a producer and a broadcaster within an organisation was deeply ingrained. Scheduling was part and parcel of that process. S4C's role was limited. They had no say in our editorial and production discussions before a programme was transmitted, but frequently there was an exchange of views after a programme was shown. S4C had a very different relationship with the independent producer. If a programme idea was accepted and commissioned directly by their programme executive, and its costing approved and the budget allocated, there was direct input and control on the finished programme. S4C would have liked to have seen that procedure and control at the BBC. It was an uneasy peace in the early days.

It took me a long time to take on board S4C's concept of promoting and marketing its service. It was aggressive, colourful and inventive. All the publicity material used on air, in the press, on billboards and buses, implied that S4C was responsible for making every programme broadcast on the channel. Rarely mentioned to the wider public was the notable contribution, in terms of hours, programmes and finance, made by the BBC and HTV. We were all attempting to safeguard our 'little patch' within the bigger scenario. Eventually, with the passage of time, the climate of suspicion eased, and the search for supremacy relaxed. Trust and respect took over. We were there to make the new channel, S4C, a success, and so it proved to be.

Three

Side by side with the excitement of planning programmes in Welsh for the new S4C channel, there was a deep-seated concern for our English output. No longer would non-Welsh-speaking viewers have to view programmes they couldn't understand, but it was imperative that we broadcasters made more programmes in English that would reflect the political, cultural and social aspects of the Welsh community and also provide a platform for new talent, writers, performers and artists. Funding for our ten-hour contribution to S4C was assured. Any expansion in English, an extra hour a week was initially proposed, also needed extra funding. This was the early eighties, and the licence fee, which had already remained level for two years, was likely to remain for a further two. Such financial stringency meant cuts rather than expansion. However, given the profound changes in the provision of television programmes in Welsh, a small amount of money was released by London to re-launch BBC Wales television as an English-only service.

Funding for network programmes from Wales had been maintained, and the early eighties had been splendid years for network drama, with Elaine Morgan's *The Life and Times of Lloyd George*, a nine-part series produced and directed by John Hefin. It had been two, if not three, years in planning and production, and proved to be one of BBC Wales's most popular and successful drama productions, with a strong performance by Philip Madoc in the title role. The catchy music, 'Chi Mai', was an inspired choice, an immediate hit, and it went straight to the top of the charts, winning a Gold Disc. John Hefin, as Head of Drama, was involved in two other productions: *Ennal's Point*, a drama series about a lifeboat community, written by Alun Richards, attracted good audiences, and Kenneth Griffith's personal view of the life and times of Tom Paine, *The Most Valuable Englishman Ever*, provoked a strong reaction.

The establishment in Wales has never fully acknowledged John's television portfolio of drama productions in Welsh and English during two decades. Perhaps he was ahead of his time. He was a creative television man whose production-and-directing skills did not carry the prestige or the authority of those who work in the theatre. Nevertheless, there are few, even today, who could match the originality of productions such as *Bus to Bosworth*. Kenneth Griffith told the story with inimitable force and humour to a group of children travelling by bus from Pembrokeshire to middle England. It relates how Henry Tudor's army marched from Dale in Pembrokeshire to Bosworth in Leicestershire, to defeat Richard III and to claim the throne of England. Then came *Grand Slam*, the riotous drama adventure of four rugby stalwarts, played by Hugh Griffith, Windsor Davies, Dewi Morris and Sion Probert, who undertake a journey to Paris to witness Wales winning the last rugby match of the season, to claim the title.

Visiting John's office to discuss programme ideas was like entering a magic emporium, a fantasyland furnished with the flotsam of discarded props from television sets, each piece carefully placed to evoke a personal romantic kingdom of memories in which magic stories could be told. Chief script editor, Gwenlyn Parry, who had combined with John to write *Grand Slam*, and light-entertainment television producer, Rhydderch Jones, a raconteur and writer, often sparked those stories. Gwenlyn and Rhydderch were two of John's closest friends, and they became the most outstanding playwrights of their generation. It was a partnership that created the vintage comedy series, *Fo a Fe*, starring the late-lamented actor and entertainer, Ryan Davies, but their prodigious output of work also included many single plays for television and the theatre. I remember Gwenlyn's *Saer Doliau* and *Y Tŵr*, and Rhydderch's *Mr Lolipop* with leading actors Dame Flora Robson and Charles Williams, and *Lliwiau*, a story woven around the snooker table, but best of all I remember their company. At times, they were outrageous and funny, at others, serious and thought provoking, but always stimulating, and always, especially on Friday afternoons, their ideas were washed down with red wine. Gwenlyn and Rhydderch died within a year of each other, in the early nineties, still far too young, in their fifties, and at their peak. Wales still feels the loss.

The schedule for BBC Wales television was as rich and as varied as was possible, given our limited resources. It was headed by a Tom Jones entertainment series. Gareth had viewed the series earlier in the year, at the Cannes MIP television festival, a market place for buying and promoting programmes from around the world. The cost of this particular ten-programme series, made in Canada, was within our budget. Tom was in his prime. We had a winner, so much so that Gareth used every ounce of persuasive guile to negotiate the right to have a different cover from the rest of the UK, for the Wales edition of the *Radio Times*. This was, in our estimation, a wondrous breakthrough. It was seen by those in London to be an unnecessary fragmentation of the one BBC, a sort of thin edge of a wedge, which carried the warning: 'Never to happen again'. The brave Editor held firm, and a full frontal, medallioned photograph of Tom, seemingly gyrating in full song, appeared on newspaper stands in Wales.

Before transmission, I travelled to Hollywood with producer John Watkin, and PA Brenda Thomas, to film an extended interview with Tom at his home in Hollywood. It was scheduled to herald the new series. This was, for me, the culmination of a dream, which had been held in suspension since my highly developed passion for the cinema became an obsession during my growing-up years at Aberystwyth. The tinsel of Hollywood was about to become tangible, and I hoped to re-live childhood fantasies of life in glorious Technicolor with the stars in Bel Air, Sunset Boulevard and Malibu.

I was not disappointed. I was a child at heart, but we were brought sharply down to earth by the hard reality of life in Los Angeles, when the taxi driver taking us from the airport to our hotel swerved sharply. He had heard Brenda ask what – to us – was a normal and respectable Welsh enquiry, 'Where do you come from?' He turned ninety degrees in his driving seat at the shock of such a personal question, to look her straight in the eye before making this challenge: 'Hey Ma'am. Don't do that. D'you wanna fanny full of fenders?'

Tom Jones lived in Dean Martin's old house in Bel Air. It was like a fortress: a high, red-bricked wall festooned with spikes and lights surrounded the mock Tudor, nine-bedroom mansion. Entry was only possible through high-wired, electrically coded doors. Tom was inside, waiting to greet us, his gold chain and medallion glinting in the high, Californian afternoon sun, on a chest of rippling muscles. He walked towards us, wearing a pair of tight shorts. I kept my eyes fixed on the shining torso.

'Come in. Good to see people from Wales.'

We entered a large garden, where the old telephone box from Pontypridd took pride of place by the swimming pool. He took us around the shady garden of mature trees and bushes, which hid sculpted effigies of large dogs, seated, standing, lying, eyes wide open, tongues hanging out, as if waiting in anticipation for the celestial whistle. Dean Martin had long since abandoned them, and Tom mumbled, 'I don't have the heart to move them'.

Filming in the house was not permitted. 'Security, see'. Tom was amiable, articulate and hospitable. We filmed the hour-long interview near the swimming pool, in the afternoon sun, and as we came to the end of our stay, his body language changed swiftly and remarkably. A young, long-limbed, lithe blonde young lady had entered the garden. A show biz reporter from San Diego was obviously about to try to discover Tom's innermost secrets. My fantasy was demolished by a look. There was no contest. I had to make do with a reality visit to the *Jaws* film set at Universal Studios.

We were far from satisfied with the number of English programmes we were able to make, especially during the first weeks of S4C. We had neither the finance nor the resources to reflect all the aspirations and ideas of our producers. Neither could we fulfil the concerns of interested viewers who believed there was a linguistic imbalance in our output. We mixed new programmes with repeats. In addition to Tom Jones, a series called

Focus on Rugby was an appreciation of world-class rugby, the last contribution by Carwyn James to television, and we repeated a series of films by the distinguished producer John Ormond, but we relied on our network commissions to supplement the output. Two major network events occurred during my first eighteen months as Deputy, which were significant as major outside broadcasts for different reasons. The visit of Pope John Paul II to Cardiff was one of these, and, the following year, 1983, the launch of the first *Cardiff Singer of the World* competition.

The papal one-day visit began with the arrival at Cardiff airport, and included the Mass in Pontcanna Fields, with an estimated congregation of a quarter of a million people, a tour of Cardiff in the Popemobile, a Youth Rally at Ninian Park and the final departure from the airport. It was a massive, complex undertaking, and our outside broadcast resources were stretched to the limit. To maximise our coverage, we proposed exploring the possibility of using an outside camera unit from HTV. Eventually, both managements agreed terms and costs. The unions disagreed. They were not prepared to work alongside a unit from a commercial company who operated different rates of pay, conditions of service and working practices. These were sensitive issues between the public and private sector workforces and, given the Government's intentions regarding the unions, this was no meeting place.

It was deadlock as the deadline approached, and during a last crucial meeting, we met once more across the boardroom table. Following a brief discussion, the union representatives retired to consider once again a list of proposals and guarantees. When we resumed, it seemed the majority of union branch officials would not negotiate an agreement. Then, a committee member, Ralph

Evans, a member of the BBC house staff team, took centre stage without warning, and began to speak. Ralph was known as a story-spinner and a leg-puller, but that morning he made an emotional and impassioned plea to his 'comrades' to rethink and to reconsider their objections.

'This is an historic visit, without precedent,' he said. 'Cardiff is to be the focus for the world's Catholics. It is an opportunity for everyone in the television industry to work together in a meaningful way.'

The room folded into deep silence. Someone cleared a throat. Geraint and I waited, bowled over by the emotional charge, until, one by one, union members agreed to negotiate, and we reached a working understanding.

The day of the Pope's arrival, a bright, sunny June day, when the avenue of trees in Cathedral Road sparkled in spiritual splendour, was a feat of organisation and logistics, masterminded for television and radio by John Stuart Roberts, Head of Religion, and director Huw Brian Williams. It was the largest, most sustained outside broadcast ever undertaken in Wales and from dawn until dusk, cameras and microphones placed in all parts of the city captured historic pictures and sounds. At the end of the day everyone was well pleased. John Watkin, who had ensured that every member of staff, wherever they were posted in the city, was fed, watered and made comfortable, mused in his own inimitable way on the event's memorable proceedings, 'I know where every lettuce leaf has gone.'

John Watkin played his part in the second outside broadcast event, too, *Cardiff Singer of the World*. A year earlier, he had returned to Cardiff from Brunei, where he had spent four years setting up a new television service financed by the Sultan. One of the benefits of working for the BBC was secondment abroad, to widen experience in interesting posts. Before his stay in Brunei, John had worked as a radio studio manager and children's television producer. He was a doer of energy and ebullience. Even his walk was a restless movement forward, striding five paces in front of every group, propelled by a need to be before his time. He and I originated from the same 'patch of land' in Cardiganshire and, at heart, John remained a countryman, transplanting the values and traditions of rural Wales onto his life in the city. He was appointed Head of Information and Press Relations on his return from Brunei, and I was to work closely with him on many projects in the eighties.

Cardiff Singer of the World was such an event, first staged in July 1983 as a biennial competition for young singers on the threshold of their careers. The brainchild of Mervyn Williams, the Head of Music, and Controller, Geraint Stanley Jones, it aimed to reflect the best of Wales and its vocal traditions; it was a showcase for the splendid, newly-opened St. David's Hall, and provided a fruitful partnership with Welsh National Opera. There would be one week of concerts, to include five rounds of competitive singing, culminating in a final on the Saturday.

A year earlier, the idea was submitted for the BBC 2 network and it received immediate backing from the Controller, Brian Wenham, who saw immense possibilities for his channel. He loved opera and he saw the competition as an accessible tournament for his viewers. After all, he had transferred a snooker tournament *Pot Black* to the television screen. The one-time minority sport, played on a rectangle of green baize, became a competitive series, which was as compelling as any tennis contest on Wimbledon's centre court. During one of our editorial meetings on our singing contest, Brian drew a master plan for television. He scheduled programme highlights for the competitive concert rounds, and a promise for the final of a live three-hour transmission on Saturday night.

Mervyn and I visited Copenhagen, to attend a European Broadcasting Union Music Committee meeting, to sell the competition to other television organisations. We were dependent on their co-operation for the selection of singers and also for giving the event television exposure in Europe. Planning took over a year, and one of my tasks was to head an organisational group from all aspects of the team: programme production, resources, design, costume, engineering, press and marketing, to ensure we kept to the timetable. John Watkin and Iwan Thomas worked tirelessly at marketing; six concerts by unknown singers was a tall order at the box office, but through their efforts, the hall, whether it was full or not, provided a warm atmosphere for competitors. The final was a sell-out and the rest is history. Karita Mattila, the glorious soprano from Finland, the first singer on stage in the first round, was the first winner. She went on to a glittering career, as have ten other winners. The year 2003 saw the eleventh competition, an event that has remained central to the music scene in Wales.

However, those early years were not without administrative incidents and were, for me, another sign of the changing structure of television. Mervyn Williams, Head of Music, left the BBC to establish an independent company, Opus 3. He became restless with the BBC's growing financial restrictions, its slowness, its bureaucratic stonewalling and its outmoded working practices. A man of drive, ideas and conviction he became a major entrepreneur in the industry. In addition to the production company, he developed a successful technical editing and graphic resource business that he called Derwen.

By the mid-eighties, the independent sector was growing and making a distinctive contribution to Channel 4 and S4C schedules. The BBC was instructed to change its 'in house' practice and acknowledge that independent producers had a place in its schedules. It was instructed to commission twenty-five per cent of its programme-making activity from the sector, and on that basis, Mervyn felt that his company was in a position to bid for the right to produce future *Cardiff Singer of the World* competitions. It was his creation and he had nurtured and developed it. These were sensitive times, but the event had been produced and financed with all the disciplines and skills of 'in-house' practitioners. It was a BBC team production, not one made by another company 'for the BBC'. Mervyn was adamant that he would not remain involved unless he was in control. It was a stark choice, a point of principle and one of the darkest mornings in my managerial experience.

It ended without appearing to descend into direct confrontation, but we failed to reach a deal. Mervyn had initially conducted the argument in familiar pose, without shoes on his feet, curled up in a chair, his hand holding his chin and cigarette, occasionally stressing a point by putting coins on the table and moving them into position, like a General explaining the aims of an army manoeuvre.

I have no doubt he walked out of my office that morning seething with anger at my decision to keep *Cardiff Singer of the World* a BBC production. I had always had a cordial working relationship with him. I had admired his work and appreciated his eccentricities. He had transformed television music programmes, mounting performances of the great oratorios, *Elijah* and *Messiah*, and a series marking the 250th anniversary of Haydn's birth. We had many long and regular lunches – part of Mervyn's staple diet – to discuss the BBC's role in an increasingly commercial environment, but our discussion that morning was not free-ranging, it was vigorous and explicit. Sadly, as a result, the cordiality towards me cooled from that day.

I put that kind of fracture to one side and moved on to find other personnel. I began by inviting Anna Williams to be the event organiser. Experienced and efficient, Anna had worked on music programmes with Mervyn as his PA and was one of the three people initially involved in the Opus 3 company, but she longed to extend her activities and to freelance in other directions. This contract gave her two years' work together with added responsibilities. It was a big undertaking but her organisational and administrative skills, plus her understanding and concern for singers, has since turned *Cardiff Singer* into the Rolls Royce of vocal competitions.

We now needed an Artistic Director, a music specialist and an experienced television practitioner to put a gloss on the screen presentation. Humphrey Burton, the former Head of BBC Music and Arts, had won many international awards, including an Emmy and three BAFTAs. He was chairing a European Broadcasting Union music conference when I met up with him during a Cannes conference, and Iwan Thomas and I managed to persuade him to lead the artistic and television production teams. At first, he hesitated. The main obstacle was his wish not to undermine, or damage, his relationship with Mervyn. I hardly think it did. They had too much respect for each other.

Humphrey's experience soon became obvious. He re-fashioned the stage design and presentation at St. David's Hall. He nurtured a young team of directors, giving them new insights and cajoling them to be confident and adventurous. He also respected our wish that the major global event, produced for television in Wales, should invoke a sense of place.

Four

The opportunity to be involved in radio and television production remained, albeit sporadically, despite my managerial responsibilities. In the early eighties, Max Boyce – his stage and television entertainment shows already a resounding success – turned his attention to feature programmes. He teamed up with an independent company, Opix Films, to make a series of six programmes for Channel 4. These were designed to follow Max's progress as he learnt how to play American football with the Dallas Cowboys in Texas. He trained hard until he was pronounced physically fit enough to face the Green Bay Packers in a friendly match. He carried Number 10 proudly on the back of his shirt as a tribute to the great fly halves of Welsh rugby, Cliff Morgan, Barry John and Phil Bennett, but the significance was lost on his team members, who had no notion of the proud tradition of the game back home. One player, his body encased in protective pads and straps, perplexed and intrigued, was to ask, 'Why is it that people who play rugby in Wales haven't got any front teeth?'

He was even more perplexed when he heard Max's reply, 'It's to stop them biting each other.'

The Cowboys narrowly lost, but the series, which recorded every bruising training session and crunching tackle, as Max tested himself to painful limits, was pronounced a success.

Stuart Littlewood, Max's agent, was anxious to develop this aspect of Max's career, and we began discussing the possibility of another series. After all, BBC Wales had developed all his network entertainment shows and given the warm, effervescent performer a platform to show his particular brand of humour. The title *Dallas Cowboys* sparked another idea. In the next series, Max would learn the high-risk skills of becoming a cowboy and a rodeo rider in America's Wild West. This was to be a co-production between BBC Wales and Opix Films. It involved our film crew plus other resource personnel working with an Opix producer and director. When the programme and broadcasting rights had been settled, I was to be executive producer, safeguarding the BBC's agreements during the weeks of production.

I flew to Colorado to see Max after a week of hard training, using muscles he never dreamed he possessed, getting himself ready and fit to take part in the premier rodeo in America, The Cheyenne Frontier Days. In this week-long festival, every cowboy worth his saddle wanted to pit his skill and courage, riding those wild broncos and bulls and lassoing strong young steers. My air flight in a twenty-seater plane from Denver to Cheyenne was weighed down with huge, hard men clothed in thick blue denim, smelling of leather and dubbin, drinking beer and whiskey, already finely tuned for a week of 'a-hooting and a-hollerin'. I was not dressed for the part. I was not a denim person and my feet refused to enter cowboy boots.

One large, tall, blond hunk, called Brad, put me right. It was the custom, if not an unwritten rule, that everyone attending a rodeo wore a cowboy hat. No hat, no drink of Red Eye at the bar, and no rodeo either. Then he asked me my name. I told him, 'Teleri'.

He didn't blink, he didn't smile, but in a deep voice that would have stopped a Brahma bull in his tracks, he proclaimed, 'Ma'am, I'll call you Sue. Everyone in Cheyenne will call you Sue.'

I very nearly adopted it after a lifetime of difficulty with misspelling, mispronunciation, and people's inability to determine whether Teleri was male or female.

When Stuart Littlewood saw his prize performer tossed in the air above the arena, a mere four seconds after being released from Chute 3, he sped to the nearest telephone, to double the life assurance. It was a testing experience; Max did not flinch, not even when he rode a huge, twisting, bucking animal called Bonecrusher, but the whole project very nearly came to a tragic end when a Brahma bull jumped the arena fence and rampaged through the crowds. A couple of cowboys tried valiantly to lasso his horns, even his back legs, but the wild-eyed bull raced onwards, kicking and bucking high in the air in fright. We were all standing, unaware, waiting to film the next sequence when the cry 'Bull! Bull loose! Bull loose!' cut across the noise of the afternoon merriment. I sprang from a standing start, high and straight onto the back of a lorry, to cower there until the mayhem subsided. I lifted my head to see the crowd surrounding a figure crumpled on the ground.

It was Brenda, our PA. The bull had hit her on the side as she had raced for cover. An ambulance quickly arrived and I took her to hospital. After a series of examinations and X-rays, they diagnosed severe bruising, a sprained knee, a broken rib and severe shock. Before we left, it was my Access account that was in a non- recovery situation. Brenda had survived a frightening incident and we returned home, leaving Max and the film crew without their PA, to continue filming for the remaining week. Brenda and I flew first class, to ease her aches and pains – my one and only journey in such comfort – and she slowly and stoically recovered. The series was a marked success. Of course, it had been 'for real'.

Making BBC Wales relevant to viewers in Wales and creating a credible, comprehensive service with a sense of community and identity was by no means easy. We were not properly funded to match the range of the ten-hour television contribution in Welsh for S4C, and apart from the daily news programme, *Wales Today*, little was produced for peak-time, pre-nine o'clock audiences. Traditionally, we had been strong in documentary, music and drama, and these were often transmitted at later times in the evening schedule. Television had concentrated on the serious, more highbrow side of programme-making. Good programmes are the product of teams of people from many disciplines, who exchange ideas and refine arguments to achieve high levels of creativity. Live sport is popular and entertaining. Coverage of rugby matches in Wales had achieved high levels of production and directing skills, because for eight months of the year producers, directors, cameramen and others were maximising their abilities every week. However, we lacked the cutting edge, and the appropriate production and resource skills for making other popular peak-time programmes.

I shared my concern one evening with Julia Smith who went on to create *EastEnders*, but who at that time was overseeing the production of the BBC Wales popular series *District Nurse*, with Nerys Hughes in the starring role. Julia was tough, tenacious and uncompromising, with a long record in theatre production, and in television popular drama, after establishing the nursing series *Angels*.

Ferociously demanding, she pushed everyone to the limit.

'It's too cosy here,' she told me that night, after a stormy meeting with a stubborn resource manager.

He was a master stone-waller. He had developed the ability to deal with every request to try something new by settling his face into thinking mode, lowering his eyelids, having a long intake of breath, followed by another long pause, presumably for more thinking, and concluding, almost always, with the words, 'Not possible'. With Julia in charge of production, he was forced to cut out all negative thoughts, to find solutions and to make everything possible, as soon as possible.

I welcomed and admired her approach, although many did not. Too hard, too pressurised, they said, but at the point when we were developing other projects for her in Wales, she was whisked away to London to devise a new drama soap to compete with ITV's *Coronation Street*. She and writer Tony Holland called it *EastEnders*, and for twenty years and more, it has anchored the BBC 1 schedule at peak time. Julia may have been a worrier and an obsessive workaholic, but she had an acute sense of audience. BBC Wales needed just that: a strong, popular and sustained style of general programming to balance the more serious offerings. We could then develop a closer relationship and identity with viewers.

I persuaded Geraint and Gareth that we should recruit and train a clutch of young directors, an investment for the future, who would provide us with new energy and a fresh impetus. We recruited six, and by the time they had completed their training and gained experience directing a range of programmes, an opportunity came to put ideas into action. Michael Grade,

Controller BBC 1, the arch-scheduler, decided to reorganise the early-evening schedule of programmes. He recognised the pulling power of the newly bought Australian soap, *Neighbours*. In order to attract viewers to daytime television, he placed an episode at lunchtime, and repeated it after children's programmes, before the six o'clock news. That decision created a major scheduling problem for us. *Neighbours* was to be transmitted in the slot allocated to *Wales Today*. Moving the news programme to a later time, after the six o'clock news, narrowed the time gap between the two transmissions, *Wales Today* on BBC 1 and *Newyddion* 7 for S4C (at seven o'clock). They were both produced from the same small studio, using the same set, and the same resources, but the teams producing them were totally different, and the later programme in the Welsh language needed a minimum of thirty minutes to set up, rehearse and coordinate production. We solved the problem by completely reorganising the early-evening television schedule for viewers in Wales, so that followers of *Neighbours* would not be disappointed. Neither would the *Newyddion* 7 production team. The exercise in complex logistics left us half an hour to fill. We mounted a variety of new and different programmes, including a series of personal interviews hosted by Cliff Morgan; an effective and imaginative health education series produced by Barry Lynch, *Don't Break Your Heart*, and I recall, too, the pace and vigour of *Juice*, our first attempt at winning young viewers.

That exercise merely emphasises the logistical problems the process of re-scheduling can cause, especially when you are dealing with the production needs of programmes in two languages. There is also the importance of providing a coherent service for viewers who don't want to miss their favourite programmes. Network Controllers, on the other hand, disliked our power and ability to opt out of their schedule to transmit locally produced programmes, claiming that network programmes lost audiences. The arguments and criticisms used were often based on the critical mass theory of television. The size of the network creative unit was considerably larger than the team resource of a region; and there was the belief that sustained high-quality programmes could not be delivered by small teams of people, and below a certain financial base. It was not a level playing field.

The London attitude was never more apparent than during coverage of International rugby matches when Wales was playing in Cardiff Arms Park. BBC Wales had developed high levels of expertise in our coverage of rugby games, and the director, Dewi Griffiths, was universally acknowledged to be among the very best in television. His positioning of cameras, his direction of angles and shots, his reading and understanding of the game to anticipate movements, coupled with close-ups of incidents and action, added to the pleasure of watching matches on television. Dewi had refined his technique of directing the complex game for television through his work covering club rugby, week after week, for BBC Wales. It was a different story for network coverage of International matches from the Arms Park. Dewi directed the outside broadcast crew, but *Grandstand* would only allow their own commentary teams to be heard on air. We believed we had our integrity and identity to maintain, and we insisted that the voices of our regular commentators should be heard for International games from Cardiff, despite many accusations of wastefulness and of unnecessary 'doubling up' of resources. Reporting stories for network television news programmes brought similar experiences. A major news story breaking in Wales would bring reporters and correspondents from London streaking to the scene, rehearsing the pronunciation of Welsh place names, merely to interpret the story for the network, while our reporters, who had covered the story for *Wales Today* and other news programmes, stood by. It was a two-tier system. It was also silly, wasteful and arrogant. Thankfully, over the years, that practice slowly disappeared, and now knowledgeable correspondents based in regional centres regularly contribute to all news programmes.

The authority of our Welsh-language news service on radio and television was severely tested during the Falklands war in 1982. International stories were often difficult. Finding Welsh speakers in different parts of the globe to give eyewitness accounts was a problem, but never insurmountable. In the South Atlantic, interviews with Patagonian descendants of the first settlers, who spoke Welsh and Spanish, brought a different perspective and dimension on the conflict. They regarded themselves as Argentinians, and they gave an individual point of view of their government's action. I'm not sure Mrs Thatcher realised the significance of those reports.

'The Falklands factor was the spirit of a new age,' so spoke a triumphant Prime Minister as victory was confirmed. A year later, in 1983, she swept into her second election, winning a huge parliamentary majority of 144 seats. For the first time, a complete radio and television results and analysis service was mounted by the BBC in Welsh, a feat of sustained organisation and logistics that kept viewers informed of up-to-the-minute declarations and results.

Within a few months of the election, miners' leader Arthur

Scargill led his union out on strike, an action that was to have a devastating effect on the social and economic life within communities in Wales. It brought into focus the anger and anguish of the great strikes of the twenties and thirties, and it polarised opinion. Issues and events dominated news programmes for a year: the violence, the hardship, the fighting rhetoric, the flying pickets, the scenes of convoys of lorries on the M4 carrying imported coal to power stations, and the tragic death of a taxi driver on the A470 near Pontypridd, when a brick was thrown at his car from an overhead bridge. The driver was thought to be taking strikebreakers to work. Moreover, who will forget the moving images of the long march by Maerdy colliers when their mine, the last in the Rhondda, closed for good two years later?

March 1984, the month when the strike began, was memorable for me for a very different reason. It was when I made a journey of a lifetime to India, to film an interview with Mrs Indira Gandhi, the Prime Minister. Some of the footage from that film had a fateful quality about it. Six months later, Mrs Gandhi was murdered by two Sikh guards outside her home, and our filmed interview, the last she recorded, was shown around the world.

The visit was arranged through our association and friendship with Shyam Verma, who presented a weekly radio series in Hindi and Urdu for the Asian community in South Wales. This community had grown during two decades, and many who settled in Cardiff, women in particular, were lonely, cut off, and unable to speak English. Shyam had settled here in the early sixties. He had left Bihar to find work, first as a bus driver and then, as he became more confident, he found employment in business and community affairs. Within a short time, he was involved in the city's political life; he became a leader and spokesman for the Asian community in Cardiff, and was elected to the city council, while, at the same time, studying for his university degree in politics and the law.

Shyam was a proud Hindu who enjoyed Western ways. He prospered as a businessman. Knowledge and enlightenment were important to him.

'I am the true product of the Raj,' he would say, his body shaking with inner laughter. 'I learnt fast,' and his smooth-skinned face would break into a wide smile.

I can recall walking with him through the high colonnade in Connaught Square, Delhi, on a hot sunny morning, Shyam dressed immaculately in a three-piece navy suit, straight-backed, proud, a gold watch-chain spanning his chest between two waistcoat pockets. He stopped suddenly, to lift his foot onto a cardboard box. A small boy, no more than ten years old, began polishing his shoes. Shyam talked to him, giving him his full attention, and, when the job was finished, handed over a few rupees, far more than the boy expected. We walked on.

'I told him,' Shyam said, 'this was his beginning in business. He must give some of the money to his mother. The rest he should save. To be successful, you should look after your parents and work very hard.'

The trappings of Shyam's success were in his lifestyle, and he enjoyed it. He lived well and expensively with his wife Babette. Evenings around their dining table in the large house in Cyncoed were filled with political and business talk, but he never forgot his roots. The feudal and impoverished land of his birth in Bihar was never far from his thoughts. He kept in close touch with his family and friends, and his political connections encompassed the Gandhi family.

Shyam was the guide who helped us understand the complexity of Indian society, and its political and cultural aspirations. John Watkin was again the producer, with Brenda as PA, and the film crew was led by the immaculate cameraman, Tom Friswell. We travelled extensively during our three-week visit, and we saw Mrs Gandhi at work in her political office, chairing a cabinet meeting, addressing a huge gathering of 50,000 people, and at her twice-weekly morning meeting – the Darshan – with her constituents. She was born to rule; she was the daughter of Pandhit Nehru, first Prime Minister of India after independence. During our journeys, we witnessed her changing moods, her capricious manner, and her autocratic demeanour and observed how her courtiers fawned around her. She was at her most natural with her family, when we joined her for afternoon tea on the lawns of her home, No. 1 Safdarjang Road in Delhi, with her son, Rajiv, his wife, Sonia, and their two children.

We filmed the extended interview in one of the main reception rooms of her official residence, almost next door to her private home. Simply furnished, it was almost bare, but for one large, pale green armchair, placed strategically against the french windows with two, much simpler, high-backed cane chairs facing it. Mrs Gandhi had agreed to join us at three o'clock in the afternoon, when she would be free, having first participated in an important debate in parliament on the growing unrest in Amritsar. The debate overran and we waited in the growing heat and humidity of an Indian afternoon. As is often the custom in India, the room suddenly filled with men, who had appeared as if summoned by a magical semaphore, each one formally dressed in a pristine white suit, standing patiently to greet their leader.

John Watkin, not always the most patient of men, began pacing up and down, and his face already a shiny, russet red from exposure to the high-noon sun, became redder and redder with worry and tension. Suddenly and silently, forty minutes later, the french windows opened, and unannounced, a diminutive, graceful figure dressed in a beautiful green and cream silk sari, glided through to sit in the huge, green armchair throne. One of the aides placed a call button on the arm of the chair, bowed and retreated backwards out of the room. The assembled throng took the cue and, in backward formation, left as silently as they had entered. The room had emptied except for the remarkable presence on the green throne.

She smiled, adjusted her sari, and said, 'I'm sorry to have kept you. The debate continued longer than expected. Have you had tea?'

It was at this point that John Watkin, coping with feelings of relief and nervousness took two steps forward to face Mrs Gandhi. He leant down, a smile from Wales on his lips.

'Thank you, Prime Minister,' the distinctive Cardiganshire accent emphasising the 'r' sound as he spoke the words 'Prime Minister'. 'Thank you,' he said again, the anxiousness more pronounced this time. He leaned ever lower, to look at her, eye to eye. 'Now, Mrs Gandhi *fach*,' he said, 'you'll be all right with us. Teleri and I both come from Cardiganshire.'

I'm not sure Mrs Gandhi needed that kind of encouragement from the cunning Cardis, but she inclined her head.

'How kind. I understand.'

That was more than I did, I must admit. She did not want to see my questions beforehand, unlike many politicians, but she was forthcoming and gave us detailed views and policies on the problems of rural communities. We filmed much of the illustrative material in remote villages north of Delhi, and I remember the pride on the faces of one farming family who were producing gas for light, and power for cooking, from fermenting chicken manure. We also saw small businesses and banks at work, and experienced a wonderful evening in Moradabad, the capital of brass making, where the local soothsayer told me, 'You will be married one day'. I didn't pay him.

Our film was not intended as a portrait of the Prime Minister, but was designed to let us hear her views on the problems of rural communities and self-sufficient practices, but events that year were so significant that the remit had to be extended and changed. During the spring (June 1984), after we had returned home, Mrs Gandhi sent army troops to the Punjab, in order to quell the unrest by Sikh separatists, but the military assault on the Golden Temple in Amritsar, the Sikh's holy shrine, only heightened the tension in a complex situation.

We had spent three weeks filming in March, when the weather was reasonable and not too hot. In August, when I returned with Shyam to Delhi, the heat and humidity were almost unbearable. The Prime Minister had agreed to extend our filmed interview and to comment on the military action, which seemed to be escalating into a dangerous confrontation with Pakistan. We met in the same room. She wore the same sari, but she apologised.

'I've just had my hair cut,' she said, and she mentioned a painful wisdom tooth. I asked her whether she feared for her own safety and thought that she might be killed. She replied that the thought that she might be killed frequently occurred to her, but she was not afraid of death. A plane was put at our disposal, so that we were able to fly to see the Golden Temple for ourselves, and I remember clearly feeling that in such a beautiful, peaceful place of holiness, there was menace in the air.

Two months later, in October, Mrs Gandhi, who had been for so long a principal point of reference for most Indians, was shot by two of her most trusted personal Sikh guards. The relevant part of our interview was seized upon by news organisations around the world, for it contained her last thoughts on the volatility in her country and her own assessment of the dangers on her life.

That film was the last I made with Brenda, the PA. She had been an integral part of so many. She was BBC Wales through and through, and, like so many others of those times, making programmes and broadcasting were her life. Committed and loyal, she knew all the rules and she knew how to bend them. If she didn't, she knew someone who did. Eighteen months after our trip to India, she decided to take early retirement but sadly, following almost thirty-five years with the BBC, she died in her sleep on the last day of her employment with BBC Wales.

Five

I had never been a public activist in the feminist campaigns of the seventies, but I hope I changed, or at least influenced, the male-dominated edifice that was BBC Wales of those years. The BBC had always employed a large number of women as secretaries, PAs, researchers, studio managers and radio producers, but they had little say in policy-making or running the service at the highest level. The Equal Pay Act and the Equal Opportunities Commission, together with the industrial transformation in Wales, changed the social and economic structure. It also challenged the macho perception of work.

As a large employer, the BBC was much exercised with the demands of the Equal Opportunities Commission, and at one point in the mid-eighties, rumours were rife that quotas would be introduced. An edict eventually arrived from London recommending that, where possible, twenty per cent of managerial posts should be held by women. BBC Wales smiled to itself. It had achieved that target well before the public announcement, with my appointment as Deputy, in 1981. It was to remain at that ratio for the next ten years, when I would be the only woman present at management meetings. In fairness, the majority of my male colleagues were not interested in gender politics, too concerned with their own careers, watching their backs, or keeping their slates clean, but, deep down, the male view dominated. It didn't really change. 'Be Mam,' they would say. 'Pour the tea,' and I learnt to show a double-edged graciousness. I poured my own.

I never really thought of myself as following a career. I had a series of jobs. Doors opened. There were chance meetings and, of course, I was lucky to have worked in a congenial environment, with people I respected and trusted. One or two did their utmost to undermine me with their obvious scepticism of my abilities, and occasionally there were sexist remarks. One of the worst occurred during a fractious discussion on a decision I had made. A bored announcer commented, 'You're very menopausal today.'

My look of disdain told him that his yearly salary increment could be in danger. I played the game on my terms. I was competitive, and I had toughened my resolve to make the most of my opportunities. I had been well taught by my broadcasting mentors – ladies of influence and talent – in the 1950s, although they did tend to accept the status quo within the organisation. They were a small proportion of the workforce, and were more concerned with production quality than with sexual equality.

Recruitment for Radio Wales and Radio Cymru changed the gender balance within BBC Wales. The number of women appointed as producers, presenters, sub-editors, reporters and researchers increased substantially, and their voices and views did much to change attitudes. The other edict for broadcasters from the Equal Opportunities Commission concerned work opportunities in broadcasting for ethnic minorities. I had appointed the first black radio producer to work in Radio Wales well before the announcement. This was Linda Mitchell, from Cardiff's dockland. She was attractive and intelligent. Educated at the Howell's Girls' School and Cardiff University, she often felt vulnerable, a person apart, unable to join in the general give-and-take. She felt herself to be different; she was different. In her mind, her colour was a barrier, and her upbringing in multi-cultural Tiger Bay occasionally emphasised her own prejudices towards identity and place. I tried to explain so many times that differences as she perceived them could be enriching qualities for programme-makers, and for influencing the community that was Radio Wales. Since those days, her career rightly flourished, and she is putting her experiences to good use as the BBC's Head of Diversity, a post that ensures that the BBC reflects the aspirations of the broad population.

Equality, for me, was a way of life, although I realised the feminist battles were only half won in 1985. I had been fortunate. I didn't miss out on marriage and motherhood and I had satisfying work. I was one of three sisters who had been given the benefit of a university education by parents who believed women should have the freedom to make choices and to be independent.

That was true of Megan Stuart, of a much later generation, another Radio Wales recruit, who had begun her career as a journalist before joining the talented breakfast programme team. She married Chris Stuart, the programme's presenter, and left her producer job to have a family. A few years later, with her two older children at school and the young one at a nursery, she took on the role of Editor, and her managerial and leadership skills soon became obvious and effective. Working and dealing with the daily pressures of the job began to dominate her life, and she was soon torn between the needs of her family and the demands of the work place. She had realised that motherhood divides women; it is rearing children and caring for them, not marriage or work, that is most important. Circumstances have changed, but twenty years ago, the majority of those who held senior managerial or executive roles were childless.

Megan found her life a constant tug of war, and one day she told me motherhood was far too important; she was missing out on precious time with her children and, regretfully, she had decided to resign and give up her job as Editor Radio Wales. As a mother, I clapped my hands in agreement. As a manager, I tried to persuade her to stay. There was no perfect solution. Often, combining work and motherhood is a necessity, but a crowded life can be full of pitfalls. It can also be a lonely struggle, and it is almost always accompanied by guilt and a nagging sense of things left undone. Many of the issues for women remained unresolved until the 1980s, despite the growth of crèches, nurseries, nannies and au pairs. The constant pressure was beginning to tell.

In the valleys, for instance, fear and anger during the miners' strike brought women into forceful action, with their support groups and political involvement. It was a new demonstration of women-power. Jill Miller, writing in 1986 in her book, *You Can't Kill the Spirit*, recalls the feeling of amazement and euphoria when women forced their way into the Abertillery 'men only' miners' institute and set up a soup kitchen. It was a formidable breakthrough, and an action I could understand and admire.

I remember holding my breath during one of the early committee meetings of the Ebbw Vale Garden Festival. I was a co-opted member because broadcasting was to play a major role in reflecting all the activities when the festival opened in 1992. At the planning stage, which took five years, we were aware of changing a landscape, by developing a steel-making site into a huge garden of leisure and events. At this particular meeting, as usual full of local authority councillors and officials, all men, we heard of a new appointment in the marketing area. It was a woman who had obtained a very senior position. This proved too much for the powerful Labour leader of Gwent County Council. His voice boomed across the room, 'Don't put her in the post. She'll only get pregnant.'

Half the men laughed at the comment, the other half waited for me to explode. The Chairman, genial Philip Weeks, with years of experience heading the mining community of the South Wales coalfield, knew how to deal with volatile, hard men who had attitude problems, and how to charm explosive women. He smiled at the meeting, didn't get involved, and moved on. His words were, 'Now, now, gentlemen. Next item.'

Equality was seldom, if ever, apparent in the Welsh rugby fraternity, especially in the hallowed committee rooms of the Welsh Rugby Union at the Arms Park. Women were not allowed inside. They knew their place, at least the wives of officials did, and a side-room was allocated to them on match days. Women executives and negotiators were no different; they had no place in the citadel of power, even on visiting days, and so our formal discussions on broadcasting rights took place at Broadcasting House. These were occasions of hard bargaining, a lot of money was invested, and the thirst for more live coverage of games was growing. Negotiations were preceded by months of lobbying at functions and dinners. We ate our way in *Grand Slam* style to successful conclusions every five years. Discussions on these occasions never wavered from two topics, rugby and more rugby; but as the steaks settled and the beer and red wine took effect, the subject would often turn to sexist stories in which women did men's bidding (and bedding).

'Forgive me, Teleri, put your hands over your ears. You know how it is.'

Of course I did, but I loved sport. Years of practice had made me tolerant, but tolerance was not a ticket to the centre of power, nor did it guarantee a coveted ticket to International matches.

Meetings and negotiations with Welsh soccer and cricket organisations were less divisive; their associations lacked the macho show of power, money and success. A volatile Welshman, Alun Evans, was Chief Executive of Welsh soccer; before taking up his appointment, he had long been a rugby man, but in his new role as the soccer supremo, he was attempting to reorganise a disparate league structure and to galvanise public interest in the national team. He found this an uphill struggle, as the sport was resting on few memorable moments of glory. Old men's eyes would shine with pride as they recalled the victorious Cardiff City team who won the the FA cup final of sixty years ago. Men a little younger would sit up straight and puff out their chests as they remembered the Wales team of 1958, taking their place in the World Cup finals in Sweden.

'We were robbed,' they would cry into their red wine.

Alun Evans and his negotiating team liked big lunches followed by suet puddings, and if, during these gastronomic feasts, conversation flagged and slumber and exhaustion took over, their memories would turn to heroic battles on the Normandy beaches during the Second World War.

I came face to face with leading lights of the game when I accompanied our commentating team to Oslo, to cover a World

Cup qualifying match between Norway and Wales, with Mike England as national coach. It was not a smooth journey. The agent responsible for all arrangements was not an expert on group travel, certainly not a large group of highly tuned sportsmen. Our expectation of a two-hour journey and an intercity flight turned into a nomadic wandering of intense frustration. When I finally got on the plane, a seasoned Welsh lady team traveller, a large blonde from Ogmore, dressed from head to toe in a woolly ensemble of glorious red and white, looked hard at me as she put her rattle in the overhead compartment, and asked provocatively, 'Follower, or fan?'

I settled in my seat, put a boiled sweet in my mouth, smiled and nodded. I was in, and I was invited to drink a tot from a bottle of whisky she produced from a large handbag, at ten-thirty in the morning. We needed several tots. We landed at the wrong airport in Oslo. Anxiousness turned to anger with another long bus journey to the hotel and training ground. The team physiotherapist and masseurs had their work cut out untangling taut ligaments and muscles. Wales lost, and the Ogmore handbag produced much larger tots on the way home.

Discussions with Glamorgan cricket authorities were courteous and leisurely, but with a hard edge to the deliberations. Network television rarely covered Glamorgan home matches; they were not a fashionable team, but we were able to negotiate an exclusive BBC Wales deal to show all their home games. We televised hours from Sophia gardens, St. Helens, Swansea, Neath and Monmouth. The second year, we went north with one-day forays to Aberystwyth and Colwyn Bay, which helped raise the profile. Live coverage brought rewards for the club, membership to the club increased, it became fashionable to 'be there' in the BBC tent, and slowly, Glamorgan began to creep up the championship table.

In the mid-eighties, the BBC's financial crisis was deepening and Alasdair Milne, who had succeeded Ian Trethowan as Director General, established a study group to find answers to some of the corporation's financial problems and shortcomings. The group, known initially as the 'gang of four', was soon recognised as 'Black Spot' as they flew in great haste up and down the land to different broadcasting centres, carrying bulging briefcases as evidence of the seriousness of their search for evidence. Geraint was a member of the group and, when the report was produced, it was radical. It called for restructuring of management, changes in operational practices and a reduction of 'in house' services. It called for a new regional directorate, led by a Managing Director who would have a seat on the Board of Management. There was a recommendation that clarified the line of command and the position of English production establishments in Manchester, Birmingham, Bristol and Local Radio stations. Alarm bells began ringing in the national regions. Scotland, Ulster and Wales saw that, at a stroke, their direct line of communication and regular meetings with the Director General would end. They believed that this was a diminution of their status, another sign of managerial tinkering and of centralization. There was no great force behind the argument. In two years, the Managing Director post was duly advertised, and Geraint Stanley Jones was appointed. When he returned to Cardiff from his Black Spot deliberations, influenced by all that he had seen of the BBC's overall operation, he set up a similar group for Wales, and invited me to chair it. We were called, rather grandly, The Wales Efficiency Study Group. I don't think we were pigeonholed into the second or third 'black spot', but we took the task of looking seriously at ways and means of making financial savings. There were four of us from different disciplines: planning, engineering and resources, and personnel. We asked all heads of departments to make presentations; indeed, anyone who felt they had a contribution to make was invited to do so. We spent weeks deliberating. We listened to evidence, we questioned views and we read reports. There were many practices that may have been right in their time, but were now almost obsolete. Those included what I termed the 'what if, in case' psychology, and the 'half man' practice. For instance, a spare person was always scheduled, and brought in to work, to service early morning radio, 'in case' of a breakdown, or to cover for anyone who had overslept, or forgot, or had too-good-a-time the night before, or any other creative excuse. The spare man sat around waiting, doing nothing, for three or four hours every day of the week, of every month. The yearly cost was substantial, and pinpointed at a stroke the cost of 'the half-man' or 'the fat in the system'. I also remember being poleaxed with disbelief when I learnt that a resource-and-service department in Wales was required to make a detailed case to London before spending as little as £3000 on a basic small white van to carry equipment. It was impossible to become responsible and accountable with that kind of restriction.

Then, there were those who knew the rules, those who bent them, and those creative people who ignored them. Our report identified over fifty restrictive working practices, which needed re-negotiating, or even abolition. In order to provide more planning flexibility for programme-makers, we recommended that more short-term contracts be offered in certain areas of activity. However, the most radical thought was to make a clear management distinction between the disciplines of the radio and television operation. When television grew and developed as the main source of entertainment, radio tended to take a back seat. Television was powerful. Radio, although considerably less costly, was effective. The efficiency group recommended changes at the top. In place of a Head of Programmes and Deputy who had responsibility for both disciplines, we believed a Head of Television and Head of Radio would sharpen the focus and provide distinctive leadership.

Change was in the air. Most of my years in broadcasting had coincided with a period of development and advance in technology, finance and programme-making, but the eighties was a period of financial stringency and political pressure. It didn't help that the relationship between Cardiff and London was a bundle of tensions. Attitudes had hardened. The top management regarded the decision to allocate £12,000,000 from the television budget to finance Welsh-language television programmes for S4C as utter folly. The BBC was also facing growing difficulties resulting from a series of political crises, which brought management into direct conflict with the Board of Governors. The Thatcher Government believed that the BBC was a hotbed of left-wing radicals. They cited a number of programme examples, such as Norman Tebbitt's attacks on Kate Adie, for what he called her pro-Gadhafi propaganda reports on the Libyan bombing raid; the investigative *Rough Justice* television programme in which conclusive evidence, gained by irregular methods, proved that a prisoner had been wrongly convicted and, most contentious of all, *At the Edge of the Union*, in the *Real Lives* series. The programme featured a day in the life of two of Ulster's Londonderry politicians, Martin

Macguiness, then Deputy Leader of Sinn Fein, and Gregory Campbell of the Democratic Unionist Party. The government had imposed a general ban on filming those who had links with the IRA, and Martin Macguiness, although an elected politician, was known to have links with the terrorist organisation. News of the programme, when it was being edited, provoked an outcry. Politicians urged the Governors to view the programme before transmission. This request was firmly resisted by the executive because such action would flout the hallowed principle that the Board did not preview programmes.

The Governors, mainly staunch loyalists, voted in favour of viewing the documentary before transmission. As a result, the programme was banned, but it was not a unanimous decision. There was one dissident voice, that of Alwyn Roberts, the National Governor for Wales, who was also Chairman of the Broadcasting Council for Wales. He argued strongly that the programme should be shown. The decision to ban fatally undermined the editorial process, over-ruled the referral procedure and, worse, endangered the BBC's political independence.

In my experience, no such conflict occurred between the Broadcasting Council and BBC Wales executives. There were many hard-hitting debates on programme standards, taste, violence, strong language and sex. Comments on programmes took place after a programme was shown, although I do remember Gareth Price admitting to a Council meeting that the original script of the drama, *The Mimosa Boys*, written by Ewart Alexander, was based on incidents in the Falklands War and contained over two hundred four-letter words. When the play was transmitted, it contained only one. 'As executives, we exchanged realism for responsibility,' said Gareth.

A former Chairman of the Council, Professor Glanmor Williams, wrote of the relationship between two sides in these terms, 'The Broadcasting Council has to realise that broadcasters must have a large degree of freedom, and should operate in response to discussion, not diktat.'

The majority of members were middle class professional people, and their views often reflected those values and attitudes. The debate on the first months of Radio Wales was harsh and vigorous. A few members, I remember, were concerned that opinion-formers in Wales were turning elsewhere; there was discussion on the philosophy we adopted for the service and the difficulty of defining its identity. Many such comments were constructive, honest and direct, and at least there was respect and understanding for what we were attempting to achieve.

In the mid-eighties, Alasdair Milne offered Geraint the position of Director of Public Affairs for the BBC. It meant a move to London and a seat on the Board of Management. The round of farewell dinners and functions seemed to go on for months, and were a real mark of affection and respect for Geraint's leadership. This was before he took the position of Managing Director Regions. The vacancy for the Controller post gave us the opportunity to play musical chairs again. Gareth moved up a place. He applied for the post of Controller Wales, was interviewed and appointed, which, in turn, left a vacancy for the Head of Programmes. From my third floor office, I could hear the noise of knives being sharpened. I had been the Deputy for four years, but I had made it known that I would not apply if the job were advertised. I knew the procedures as well as anyone but, this time, my reasoning was simple. I was in my mid-fifties, within five years of retirement, and at that age I found the thought of being questioned on my experience and my views on the future, following months of work producing an efficiency report for BBC Wales, a little demeaning. I knew that discussions were being held behind closed doors in Cardiff and London. The television and radio directorates in London were involved, because the Head of Programmes post carried the responsibility for all network activity in Wales. The Broadcasting Council Chairman was also consulted and the Council's members exercised their collective right to express views on the appointment.

Gareth, as the new Controller, asked me whether I would take the job if it were offered to me. I said 'yes' immediately, and again gave my reasons for not wanting to follow procedures. Selfish? Arrogant? Probably, and I had many other reasons. The discussions behind closed doors continued and I had no idea of the outcome. There was no news, until the next meeting of the Broadcasting Council, the last Geraint was to attend before leaving for London. Within an hour, the door of my office opened and Geraint walked in.

'Congratulations,' he said, and hugged me. I had received the full backing of the Council and the London directorates. It was a thrill. The challenges ahead were daunting. There was much to do.

Six

First, I chose my team. Most of the Efficiency Group recommendations had been accepted by BBC Wales management and, in a break with tradition, two new posts, Head of Television and Head of Radio, were established. The two people we selected were tried-and-tested practitioners who possessed leadership qualities and the experience to make things happen. They had also shown they were prepared to work with me.

Meirion Edwards was selected to be Head of Radio, a safe pair of hands who had guided with firmness and authority the Welsh-language radio service, Radio Cymru, since 1978. He and I had worked closely together in establishing new radio services, and in this new post he would be responsible for all financial matters governing radio, production, staff and resources. Total costing had come to stay.

Television was placed in the hands of John Stuart Roberts, the Head of Religious Programmes. He was an ordained minister, who had left his ministry in Cardiganshire to become an assistant producer in the religious department in the early seventies. His programme-making was of the highest quality; he had been invited to become editor for a year of the network series, *Heart of the Matter*, in London Television Centre, where his reputation as a generator of ideas and motivator of people was immediately recognised. I had no hesitation in appointing him. He was a man of strong convictions, formidable and articulate in argument. In his twenties, in his first years as a minister, he learnt to speak Welsh, not merely as a means of communication, but to be able to immerse himself in the history, literature and culture of Wales, to be a complete Welshman. He had expressed clear aspirations for television in Wales during his interview, and they were to increase the number of English programmes to be shown 'in Wales, for Wales'. Historically, we had always opted out of BBC 1 to show our programmes, but the re-configuration of transmitters now enabled us to opt out of BBC 2. It gave us greater choice and greater flexibility. The notion of a new English service for Wales, on a par with S4C, was a distant dream, but one which we constantly talked about and aimed for.

John and I spent a lot of time together in those first months, discussing, arguing and planning. He reorganised his production departments, he set up training schedules for new recruits, and he revitalised our 'on-air' presentation in order to trail our programmes aggressively. Significantly, John moved to re-name as BBC 1 Wales and BBC 2 Wales both television services seen in Wales. It was a fine distinction, but a necessary one, if we were to market a distinctive product.

Then, as programme ideas were becoming more than scribbles on paper, the cancer struck like a bolt from the blue. I was attending a Prix Italia festival in Lucca, with Meirion and John Hefin, when a bout of intense giddiness and light-headedness engulfed me. The buildings of the historic Tuscan city spun around me as I walked. I managed to hide my condition from colleagues and the feeling passed, but two days later, when we paused in Pisa before our flight home, the leaning tower tilted a little further than normal as I walked towards it. I saw the GP as soon as possible after I arrived home. He ordered me to undergo a series of blood tests and recommended later that I saw a haematologist. A series of tests and scans divulged an abnormality in my right kidney. It was a mass, or tumour, which had to be removed immediately. The registrar had already arranged with a consultant urologist for my operation to take place.

The news came as a bombshell. All of it happened in the days before and after Christmas 1986, and when he talked to me, the registrar was as reassuring and gentle as he could be, but I noticed then, and remember clearly now, that he refused to look directly at me. He seemed more comfortable gazing down at his Hush Puppies. My eyes followed his.

'Go home,' he said gently, and the right Hush Puppy twitched. 'Go home, put your affairs in order. Mr Mathews will operate next Wednesday.'

I spent the next three days shredding papers, paying bills, making a will, buying new nightdresses and putting a semblance of order on my underwear drawer. Plans for work took a back seat; I faced a more critical issue in January 1987. Was I to survive?

When I awoke from the operation, I heard the consultant's voice.

'You're one of the lucky ones,' he said, giving me the first piece of good news. As far as he could judge, the tumour was confined to the kidney. It was a primary, and the subversive cancer cells had not floated around my arteries and veins to settle as secondaries in other glands and organs. Subsequent laboratory tests on a biopsy confirmed the diagnosis. I was lucky indeed; I recovered quickly, but it took three months to get fit enough to return to work. For ten years, I went back to the hospital for regular checkups until, finally, I was discharged from the wonderful care of the urology consultant surgeon, Peter Mathews, at the University Hospital.

Nevertheless, there is a lot more to the experience of an illness like that. The diagnosis had stunned me. My body had let me down just at the point when I had reached the peak in broadcasting. The first days of feeling angry, gutted and frightened passed. I came to accept my fate, knowing I had a fight on my hands. I soon realised that a fight like this was a team effort. My family, Huw and his fiancée, Claire, a nursing sister at the hospital, together with my two sisters, Buddug and Rhiannon, were practical and comforting. They listened to my ramblings and fears and they cared. There was also my faith.

I am a regular Sunday worshipper, in the dawn stillness of St Michael's Church, Tongwynlais, a small, village church on the outskirts of Cardiff, and at Llandaff Cathedral. I usually arrive fifteen minutes early, to embrace the peace and silence before the solemnity of the eight o'clock Eucharist. That dark morning of the operation in January 1987, the fear disappeared, and I experienced a feeling of great well-being as I lay on the trolley, a deep certainty that the outcome would be successful. I was in no position to argue with the surgeon when he observed, as I regained consciousness from anaesthetic, that I had been lucky. There had been other forces of comfort and encouragement at work. My mortality had been challenged, and the time had come to evaluate my lifestyle and to pause, to begin appreciating the small happenings of each and every day. For almost a decade, since my marriage ended, I had been caught up in the social culture of broadcasting at the time. I was free, and I suppose rather lonely. I was caught up in boozy lunches, partying, gatherings in the office over a bottle of wine at the end of a working day, and long-drawn-out suppers. The pace of my life had quickened; at times it was fraught, full of anxiety; at others, it was a roller-coaster, racing on a sea of adrenalin and excitement. It was so very sociable and fun. The cancer put a brake on all of that. The demons kept on appearing and rampaging in the darkness of the night, to remind me that the cancer could re-appear without warning at any time. I needed to change my ways. I stopped smoking, I bought a bike and I swam every day before going to work. It took a year to regain my full stamina but, to this day, I have kept up the regime.

During the first weeks of my convalescence, news came of the brutal sacking of the Director General, Alasdair Milne. It sent shock waves through the BBC and beyond. The Thatcher Government had been critical of the organisation since they came into power, but in 1986, two events pointed to a decision that was to have a far-reaching effect. The Chairman, Stuart Young, died of cancer, and he was succeeded by Dukey or Marmaduke Hussey. The second was a series of television programmes that the government thought were critical of them and their policies, culminating in a Panorama special, *Maggie's Military Tendency*, which exposed alleged links between some Tories and right-wing extremist organisations. Immediately, Mrs Thatcher invited Dukey to be Chairman of the Governors. He had impeccable qualifications for the role, which was to bring the BBC to heel, and to lead the governors into exercising greater control over its activities. A bluff, gruff sort of a man, he was a former Guards officer who had lost a leg in the battle of the Anzio beachhead during the Second World War. Tall, big and hearty, leaning heavily on his stick, he had presided as Managing Director over the year-long strike at the *Times* newspaper, and seemed to be the ideal man to deal with the left-wing tendencies of the BBC. He began with the leader, the Director General, forcing a brutal and an undignified end to Alasdair Milne's tenure – a man who had spent a lifetime in the BBC, climbing the ladder as producer, editor, controller, director of programmes, managing director and Director General. He was fired, unexpectedly and directly, one lunchtime, after a routine Board meeting between Governors and management.

When I returned to work in the spring, after spending a week of sun in Crete, rumours gathered pace on who would be the Governors' next choice. Following the brutality of the sacking, they played safe and, later in the year, Michael Checkland, an accountant who had for many years been responsible for television resources, planning and finance, was appointed Director General. He, in turn, picked an outsider as his deputy, John Birt of London Weekend Television. His brief was to 'sort out news and current affairs,' the BBC's journalism, the source of so many difficulties and problems during the Milne years. John Birt, with his customary attention to detail and analysis, took a much wider programme-and-departmental remit. The era of consultants, task forces, efficiency initiatives, focus groups, internal marketing and central control was about to begin.

Meanwhile, back at my desk, I was soon involved in our annual round of negotiations with network Controllers of BBC 1 and BBC 2. These meetings were considered pivotal for the BBC Wales operation. They gave us the opportunity, once a year, to sell television programme ideas made for the networks. Expensive dramas and music programmes needed greater finance than we could provide from our budget. They also needed a wider audience, and it was equally important for the networks, for the sake of diversity, to reflect programmes from the National regions. In the eighties, it became progressively more difficult to achieve a successful contribution. It came down to a matter of finance and centralisation.

Occasionally, high-minded television moguls came on talent-spotting missions. Roger Laughton had been appointed to develop a cohesive schedule of popular programmes for daytime network television, and in order to reflect the diversity of voices, accents and skills for easy-viewing type programmes, he invited each region to suggest names of suitable presenters and reporters. From Wales, he said, he would like a woman. I gathered together compilation tapes of leading presenters at work and I sat and watched with him. He liked what he saw, especially the skills and experience shown by the popular presenter Elinor Jones of HTV. He saw her tape twice, if not three times, and then he turned his gaze from the screen to look at me.

'No, I'm sorry,' he said. 'It's her elbows you see!'

When I had picked myself up from the floor, I gathered that, in his opinion, Elinor's elbows were too mature for the proposed daytime television image.

It is little wonder that the television service was under constant pressure. Programme costs were escalating whereas budgets remained static. As a result, programmes from London production departments were protected and safeguarded, and submissions from the regions went to the back of the queue. It gave our negotiations an edge. It wasn't that we didn't have ideas, but Controllers were loath to spend outside London. They kept the money for projects where they could directly control it, and where, in their opinion, there was greater expertise.

Procedures for these negotiations were conducted with a degree of formality. We met each Controller twice a year. Meetings called Editorials took place in Cardiff in late spring. These gave an initial reaction to our ideas, scripts and developments. There was discussion on strengths and weaknesses, and about whether the idea fitted into a network's overall future transmission plan, usually covering the following year. Major drama series, concerts or documentaries were often part of long-term planning, due to their complexity, with transmission at least two years ahead. Later, in the autumn, we got together again, this time for hard bargaining in London. These meetings, called Offers, were when costs, budgets and resources for those ideas that had been initially accepted, 'in principle,' in the spring, were negotiated. It seemed a simple, straightforward procedure, but it called for a level of cunning and salesmanship of the kind often found flourishing in Tregaron sheep market. Initial enthusiasm for an idea could count for little when finance clerks and planners had done their work. When financial matters became critical, plans were delayed, shelved, or conveniently forgotten. That usually meant that money went to other, always better, projects in London production departments.

The most difficult area of all was drama. The first hurdle, quite rightly, was the script. Plays were complex to produce, when so many disciplines such as film, design, make-up and costume were involved. In addition, there was a need for technical resources, and these often sent costs soaring, unless there were rigorous controls. There were producers who planned meticulously, who completed their productions on time and within budget. Others, with unfailing charm, would apologise for every over-run, overextended resources and, worse, for being over-budget. They were the creative people, they pleaded, but a combination of charm and incompetence could not always be indulged, it damaged reputations. There was a famous production, back in the seventies, called – appropriately – *Me and My Bike,* which became such a three-year saga of delays, confusion, re-writes and re-shoots that it failed to get to the editing stage. The costs rose through all the ceilings in Broadcasting House, and the expensive production never saw the light of day or the screen, the producer maintaining that it was still 'a good idea'. He was 'on his bike' before more of his complex good ideas reached the planning stage.

Nevertheless, we had our successes. A drama production, which John Stuart negotiated with the department of religion in London, was a superb production made in Wales. *Shadowlands,* written by Bill Nicholson, was the moving story of C. S. Lewis and his wife, who died tragically of cancer. Set in Oxford, much of the action was shot in Shyam Verma's house, and he would often regale us with stories of the lead actors, Joss Ackland and Claire Bloom, sitting in his study during filming. They gave fine performances and the production won an Emmy award, and Claire Bloom won a BAFTA Best Actress award. It has since been made into a successful film and a stage play.

Inter-departmental co-operation and co-productions with other broadcasting organisations was another useful method of increasing finance for costly network productions. The process of hammering out agreements between two sides was often fraught with suspicion.

The BBC, which had a long history and reputation for the skills of its 'in house' operation, could no longer dictate terms; it was now having to compromise and work with independent directors and producers. Doing deals was not part of my make-up, but Gareth Price was in his element negotiating, giving a little and taking a little more, until a settlement was reached. These were early days, but then came the 1988 Broadcasting Bill, which required the BBC to ensure that twenty-five per cent of transmissions, the programme output, would be the work of independent producers. A large document landed on our desks: the Terms of Trade, detailed and comprehensive, with instructions on the labyrinth of regulations we were to follow in our dealings with independents. This directive had huge implications. A reduction in BBC-produced programmes meant a reduction of the workforce, and the savings gained from salaries of staff cuts would be transferred to programmes from the independent sector. It was more than a culture shock; there were real fears for the future, and morale plummeted. One could see that, from some areas, skills would be lost, and departments decimated. Suddenly, a career within the BBC was no longer a secure option; issuing short-term contracts for particular projects made the future uncertain. So it proved to be. Change was imminent. We lost 113 posts in the first tranche of reorganisation; we pared down departments, and looked again at our working practices. The BBC had been labelled overstaffed and profligate; the harsh economic strictures imposed on the public sector by the government were the crusade to make us more efficient. I recall one Friday afternoon when we said goodbye to thirty-five individuals who had been colleagues and friends for so many years.

The quest for co-producers and extra finance continued

vigorously. Two major films in conjunction with the Canadian Broadcasting Corporation, *Going Home* and *Heaven on Earth*, were made with the entrepreneur Pat Ferns striking a hard bargain for television rights. We entered into an agreement with S4C to produce two versions of one programme, one in English and one in Welsh. It was relatively easy to make two versions of a documentary, which was often a matter of translation, but a play could be complex. We called it back-to-back television. There was often a difference in emphasis between the Welsh version and the English, although the cast was the same for both. Resources, too, together with the directors and producers, were common to both, and although the experiment was considered an effective way of maximising effort and costs, it was, more often than not, artistically limiting. Subtitling Welsh-language plays in English was another aspect. Two major plays stand out in the memory. *Gwenoliaid* by Rhydderch Jones was an evocation of the war years, and the painful experiences of evacuees from big English cities, as they attempted to integrate into remote, Welsh-speaking, rural communities. The subtitled version, titled *Swallows*, shown on BBC 2 Wales, received a favourable reaction, as did a Michael Povey play, *Sul y Blodau,* or *Palm Sunday,* produced by Richard Lewis.

It was increasingly difficult in the second half of the decade to get our product on the network, drama especially. The centre often had a dismissive, even a patronising, attitude to the regions, and two Controllers with whom John and I dealt were past masters at showing it. Jonathan Powell, the former Head of Drama, had followed Michael Grade as Controller BBC 1, and Alan Yentob, Head of Music and Arts, became Controller BBC 2, following Graeme Macdonald's retirement. Jonathan Powell won awards for series such as *The Barchester Chronicles* by Trollope, and John Le Carre's *Smiley's People*. Alan Yentob had edited the acclaimed arts series *Arena*. They had many attributes, but showing a glimmer of respect for the regions was not one of them. Taking one look through his granny glasses, Jonathan Powell could make anyone feel – to borrow one of Gwyn Thomas's memorable lines – 'lower than the lino'.

At one of our ritual Editorial meetings, this time in London, the signs were ominous before it began. The office was empty. We waited. Five minutes later a planner walked in. He was a stranger to us, but planners were easy to identify. They had a worn, grey look about them, they were never without a mountain of files in their arms, and they were occasionally to be seen scurrying along corridors from meeting to meeting. The one who walked into Jonathan Powell's office that day looked like a refugee from *Dad's Army*, the sleeves of his jacket too long, his trousers too short, and he looked as though he was surfacing from a panic attack. He banged his files on the table, wiped his brow and, without so much as a hello, he settled down to make notes on a piece of paper with a superbly-pointed yellow HB pencil.

Five minutes later, Jonathan Powell rushed in and sat behind his desk, the weight of BBC schedules obviously on his mind. He coughed.

'Welcome,' he said quietly and coughed again, looking hard at the paper in front of him. He lifted his head to focus on us and then looked down again. We waited like miscreant children at school found cheating by the monitor.

The perspiring planner again noisily sharpened his yellow pencil, and we heard the quiet voice declare, 'No drama this year'.

For a moment, I thought that dramatic cuts at the centre were really taking effect, and I tried to form an intelligent reply, but all I managed was a squeak in the form of a question. 'No drama?'

'No. No drama from Wales next year.' The planner's pencil paused momentarily and then he scribbled furiously.

I came down to earth with a bump and gathered my thoughts quickly. 'But you haven't discussed any of our proposals!'

'No need to. I have no money for drama productions from Wales next year. I can't do it.'

The argument continued, it hardened, but Jonathan Powell was adamant. He had made his decision without considering our ideas. The budget had been allocated to London departmental projects. Two days later, the Broadcasting Council met in London with the new Chairman, John Parry, as national governor. As was the custom at council meetings, I reviewed the previous month's programme activities, and I ended with the bad news that it was unlikely that Wales would produce any drama for the network in the next financial year. The Controller had no money. The reaction from council members was serious concern, and when the Director General, Michael Checkland, joined the meeting an hour later, the atmosphere was one of pointed questioning and controlled indignation. Before lunch, the DG agreed to reverse the decision, determined to find money from his personal fund.

Wales had won the argument but Jonathan Powell had won the battle. Funding from the DG's fund meant an overall increase in BBC 1 drama output. It was all sweetness and light at our hastily convened next meeting and we negotiated high quality productions from Wales. Alun Owen adapted the novel *Unexplained Laughter* by Alice Thomas Ellis, with Elaine Page and Diana Rigg in leading roles; and *Heartlands*, the story of a farmer, played by Anthony Hopkins, battling against EEC intervention. It was worth the battle and we ignored the patronising gamesmanship.

Our experience with Alan Yentob and BBC 2 was a trial of patience. Supremely talented as a producer and editor, he was a disorganised administrator. He was 'minded' by a posse of planners and assistants on the sixth floor of Television Centre, who attempted to speed his decision taking, control his spending and bring order to his diary. In his new role as Controller, he had little respect for the minnows of Wales. He was a big player on a big stage, who rarely ventured further north than Golders Green. My patience was stretched to breaking point at his lack of courtesy, when he failed to turn up at the appointed time for one of our editorial meetings. I was in no mood to kow-tow to him. We waited and waited in his empty office, and, after twenty minutes, I got up.

'Come on, fellows, we're going home. We have work to do. We'll arrange another meeting, at another time, on our terms.'

We returned to Cardiff without once regretting my action, to find an urgent message from Mr Yentob asking me to call him. He was a petulant Controller, no apology from him, no eating humble pie from me, but we resolved to keep our lines of communication open and to meet again. We made two plays based on the Falklands War, *The Mimosa Boys* and *Bluff Cove*, in addition to a well-crafted and moving programme looking back on the tragedy and trauma of Hungerford, as the village recovered from the mass shooting by a gunman.

Our difficulties with networks pointed the way to another direction. John Stuart regrouped his resources and finance to commission six plays by new writers. He gave them the umbrella title, *The Welsh Playhouse*, and he invited Ruth Caleb, the respected drama producer, to take an overview on the writing and production. She had spent time in Wales, working closely with film-maker Karl Francis, on *Morphine and Dolly Mixtures*, a searing portrayal of a young girl left to cope on her own with looking after her brother and sisters when her mother died of brain cancer. Ruth was an uncompromising producer. I felt her work too often portrayed the despair of the darker side of life, but she maintained that she was not in the business of creating soft, popular drama in order to get high audience ratings. Writers for *The Welsh Playhouse* series were fortunate to have a critical and helpful producer to analyse their work, and we were fortunate, too, that her name and reputation added strength to our network proposals.

The next project was to reassess the ten hours of Welsh-language programmes we made for S4C. The channel had been established for five years when we began the process, and it was the right time to analyse its effectiveness and think about how we could improve it. First, we looked at our news output of one programme an evening, and then we thought about the artificial division between the BBC, as the provider of a nightly news programme, and HTV, who made a weekly current affairs programme. A comprehensive news service was required during the channel's hours of transmission, and we estimated we could provide shorter and sharper bulletins at different points in the schedule. We also proposed a season of investigative programmes. S4C welcomed all these possibilities and began reorganising the schedule as we reorganised production effort. Gwilym Owen, who headed our News and Current Affairs Department, was soon making changes to staff and presenters. A few doubters kicked and screamed at the thought of being moved from their comfort zones, but Gwilym was not diverted; he was fair, and too experienced a journalist to worry about too many sensitivities. Female presenters and newsreaders believed he was anti-women, and would take every public opportunity to say so. They believed they were not paid as much as men for doing the same job. I could find no evidence that this was so, and discussed it several times with Gwilym. His judgements on fees were based on experience, standards and journalism. He did more than most to encourage women to take on editorial and managerial roles, and of all his legacies to journalism in BBC Wales, he raised standards, especially in Welsh news programmes.

The most far-reaching and revolutionary decision we took during the process of evaluation was the concept of mounting a nightly soap drama. Five years after the channel was launched, viewing figures for S4C had reached a plateau.

Commentators and critics believed that the channel was unable to capture and sustain the interest of new viewers. In fairness, competition from other channels was increasing with satellite companies offering a wide choice, but S4C's problem, or part of it, was with its schedule and popular programming. Snap solutions are hard to find, but occasionally ideas come to the surface when you least expect them. We met for lunch, John Stuart, Euryn from S4C and I, to share thoughts on many points of interest between us. We often met formally, but, occasionally, we had long, informal, gossipy lunches. This time we paused to discuss the concern about audience figures and how best to attract viewers. Out of the blue, I said to Euryn, 'What you need is a daily story for the early evening. What about *Pobol y Cwm*? It's got all the ingredients, it's familiar and it's popular. We've got the resources, but is it possible?'

I'm sure I felt the earth move, then there was silence. John looked at his mushroom risotto, and Euryn had the good sense to order another bottle of house red. 'Well?' I waited.

Slowly, John muttered, a twinkle in his eye, 'Yes. It's absolutely crazy, like many of your ideas. But, yes, it IS possible.'

It's true to say we had mapped out a number of crazy ideas since we had worked together, for radio and television, and if he said it was possible, it would happen. Euryn knew it too.

Pobol y Cwm was a popular weekly drama series, included in the schedules since October 1974, and much of the action in the early days took place in an old people's home in a Carmarthenshire village close to industrial south Wales. Well-known actors who portrayed characters in a tightly-knit community became established and loved for their humour, their quarrelling and their life styles. It was the work of writer Gwenlyn Parry and producer John Hefin, who saw its popularity develop over sixteen years. They were to be crucial if the expansive new idea was to take off. By the end of that lunch, we had a plan of action. Back at Broadcasting House that afternoon, John Hefin gave his blessing, enthusiastically, and they began getting down to the nitty gritty problems of putting names against jobs, organising studios and resources, writers and directors and an operational schedule. The majority thought the whole idea crazy, a non-achievable and a non-sustainable venture, condemning it as a waste of money and resources. Could we sustain good scripts, plot lines and characterisation? Would we kill a good weekly series with over-kill by showing it nightly? Were we about to over-extend the work of writers, actors, designers, directors and producers? 'It can't be done' is a well-known expression in a large bureaucratic organisation, which can blunt and ossify progress. 'You are mad' is another one.

The plan of action was beginning to take shape, and we invited a respected television producer, Gwyn Hughes Jones, to lead the project with writer Wil Jones as chief script editor. We had entered new territory for television in this country. This was the first time a daily story for television had been attempted. Each episode, twenty minutes long, was to be rehearsed, recorded, and edited during the day, with transmission in the early evening; this provided an opportunity to include a measure of topicality in the scripts. Once the teams got to work, I began intense discussions with S4C on the question of scheduling and the time of transmission. Everyone agreed the slot should be at the same time every night, but there were some mighty arguments about the actual time of transmission. I saw *Pobol y Cwm* as a regular, popular audience-grabber at the start of an evening's viewing. S4C were determined to place it mid-evening, at the heart of the schedule. I had long realised that family viewers at peak time, after supper, with the children in bed, expected more solidity from programmes as their evening viewing progressed. A light daily serial, only twenty minutes long, would be appreciated and judged in a very different light at eight or nine o'clock. For once, I was proved right. Transmissions began at 6.40 p.m. in the autumn. The ratings soared, and *Pobol y Cwm* became the most popular programme in the channel's history.

Setting up an independent trust to make feature films was another promising venture. Channel 4 with its *Film on Four* had blazed the trail, and was reaping the benefit from its investment. *Letter to Brezhnev* and *My Beautiful Launderette* were early successes, and they were followed by the immensely popular money-spinners, *Howard's End* and *Four Weddings and a Funeral*. There was little opportunity for making feature films in Wales, and none in the Welsh language. We opened negotiations with Euryn of S4C to explore the possibility of establishing a partnership based on the Film on Four set-up. We had successfully co-produced a film, *A Penny For Your Dreams*, the story of the film pioneer William Haggar, which was shown on BBC 2 Wales, and in Welsh on S4C with the title *I Fro Breuddwydion*. It seemed the next positive step was investing in a film trust. Ffilm Cymru was born, with John Hefin relinquishing his role as head of drama to be the first Artistic Director. Work began to commission scripts, and in three years, two films were produced. At about the same time, a young entrepreneur, Berwyn Rowlands, working in the theatre at Aberystwyth, began a film festival. It soon captured the imagination and it gave the industry a real impetus. He brought dynamism and glamour to nights of first screenings, and he marketed the festival aggressively. Sgrîn Cymru expanded and gained a widening reputation, investing in new films and assisting budding directors and producers. Soon it changed its name from Ffilm to Sgrîn Cymru, and the festival moved from Aberystwyth to Cardiff.

It had been a roller-coaster of a decade, most of it dominated by television and I knew my time as head of programmes was coming to an end. I had witnessed many developments but the dream to establish an English-language television service, in Wales for Wales, remained just a dream. BBC networks remained strong and inviolate, and full scale opting out of BBC 1 and BBC 2 was not an option. John Stuart, with typical fatalistic belief and bravery, attempted for one week to reschedule programmes on BBC 2 in order to create a coherent sequence of programmes produced in Wales for transmission at peak time. It received a mixed reaction. Many viewers appreciated the effort and liked the programmes, but the majority preferred to stay with network favourites. Reform and revolution were in the air, as talk of the impact of digital technology on radio and television was opening up immense possibilities. No-one was quite sure how it would all work, but the prospect of an abundance of channels was surely hope for the future of radio and television in Wales. The dream could remain with us, vivid and alive.

1990

A new decade dawned and I was into my sixtieth year, my last working year. I should have sailed smoothly into retirement and been allowed to indulge myself just a little, to reflect with colleagues on successes and failures, the fun and friendships of almost thirty-five years in public service broadcasting. The last decade in programme management had been full of change and incident and, I think, we had made progress despite financial restrictions. I was leaving my post as Head of Programmes, giving Gareth, as Controller, the opportunity to decide whether a replacement was necessary, now that the new structure of a Head of Radio and Head of Television was working well. Given the BBC's crusade for savings, I should have been invited, nudged, even pushed to leave earlier, to have taken early retirement. Not a bit of it. I found myself caught in a series of events that ranged from the bizarre to the laughable, from the exasperating to the lamentable.

The news came as a bombshell. Gareth Price suddenly announced he was leaving. He had been appointed Controller of Broadcasting for the Thomson Foundation, a body that trains journalists in developing countries, and assists broadcasting organisations around the world to establish effective operational structures. Not once during our long working association had I thought he would leave before me. I suppose I lived in my own little comfort zone, thinking that BBC Wales would remain the same. But he was fifty, he loved travelling, and he was grasping the opportunity to change direction and to head another organisation. From February, when he announced his departure, to June, when the name of the new controller was announced, punters peddled their predictions, gambled and gossiped. I had thought I would be winding down, that I would be a bystander and an impartial observer of events. I was genuinely looking forward to retirement, and all the different opportunities to do different things that were hovering in the background. I was looking forward and feeling happy.

That didn't last long. Within a week or so of the advertisement appearing in the press, John Parry, the national governor, asked me whether I would be prepared to 'fill the gap', be acting Controller, should there be a delay in the appointment process. It was a reasonable request at that stage, and knowing something of the BBC's propensity for secret, intricate machinations when senior appointments are at stake, it did not surprise me, but it did set a few warning bells ringing in my head. Why should there be a delay? My official retirement day was not until April 1991 and there were at least eleven months to go.

Thankfully, I told no-one. Next, came a telephone call from the office of the London Regional Directorate; the caller was an assistant to Ron Neill, the Managing Director.

'As the next Controller Wales,' she said, 'I'm ringing to ask whether you would like to go to the Queen's garden party at Buckingham Palace?'

It didn't seem the moment to question her assumption of my future status, so I agreed to attend. Then, in a few days, John Parry appeared again. I paid another visit to his office, and he asked me another pointed question, this time more direct.

'Would you be prepared to take on the Controller job for two years, that is,' and there he paused to take in a long breath, 'that is, should it come to that?'

This time I was worried, really worried. I knew that my two colleagues, John Stuart Roberts and Meirion Edwards, had applied for the post but they had not received any notification. I replied that I would wait to see what happened, but if, for whatever reason, there was a delay, I would consider the request and probably do so positively. Weeks went by, and we were into Gareth's last days as Controller and the round of farewell dinners and parties. We had worked well together; he was always ready to give support and direction, and I enjoyed his company and was grateful for his friendship.

It was early June and, unexpectedly, I received an invitation to lunch in London with Ron Neill. This was a strange occasion. He was distracted, or preoccupied, reading a draft copy of his report for the BBC Annual Report to be published later in the year. I sat in silence in the taxi, and for much of the first course at the restaurant, as he corrected the proof of the report in time for the afternoon deadline. It was only when the coffee arrived that he became animated. He grabbed a spoon to make a few imaginary drawings on the white tablecloth, and in his deep, Scottish brogue, I heard that question again.

'Would you be prepared to take on the Controller job for two years should we fail to make an appointment?'

'It won't come to that,' I replied lamely, 'I will await the outcome.' As an afterthought – and I don't know why – I added, 'My health is all right.'

He could give no indication when the matter would be resolved.

'Soon, hopefully,' was all he could say, as we said our good byes.

I felt such a cheat, so unclean. John and Meirion had heard nothing for ten or twelve weeks, not even whether they had made the short list. They had applied in good faith, they were respected

BBC employees, and the least they deserved was a measure of respect in return. On the train journey home, I felt angry. I went to get myself a large gin and tonic, although I didn't need a sip of it to realise that John and Meirion were not in the running. They were not to be interviewed, and the open advertisement was a well known ploy. I went home and didn't whisper a word to anyone.

The following afternoon, a mere twenty-four hours later, there was a knock on my office door: 'The Chairman wants to see you immediately.'

I went into his office and, without raising his eyes, John Parry announced, 'Geraint Talfan Davies has been appointed Controller.'

'Fine. Good,' I answered. I smiled at him, but inwardly I could have flattened him with a hot iron. Of course, I knew Geraint had been in the frame. He had been interviewed for the post five years earlier, when Gareth was appointed, and rumours had reported that power-brokers had been hard at work trying to make deals with him since early spring. He was a journalist who had worked in newspapers, with HTV, and at the time of his new appointment, he was Director of Programmes with Tyne Tees Television in Newcastle. I sent a fax of congratulation immediately.

However, the powers that be hadn't finished with me yet. A day later, a very English voice, that of Ron Neill's PA, was on the telephone to issue one final edict on the matter.

'Since you are no longer to be Controller Wales, we're withdrawing the invitation to the Queen's garden party. All right?'

When I look back, I was more hurt than angry, and sad, too, that responsible people should find it necessary to play such dirty games, not just with me, but with John and Meirion. I told them so, but I doubt whether it had any effect and that saddened me further. I felt nothing but contempt for the emerging style of management from Ron Neill and DG Mike Checkland. I was retiring. I met Geraint Talfan Davies and was genuinely welcoming, and, at his invitation, I agreed to stay until Christmas. He could not take up the post until September, so I also agreed to become acting Controller for three months. The 'interregnum' is what they called it. I really felt it was more like play-acting. I could sit in the Controller's chair, but I had no real power. I had no say in the future and I could give no direction. Undoubtedly, the main perk of that summer was having the luxury of riding to events and functions in the official BBC Wales car.

The mood of staff during those months was difficult to define. Mostly, it was a mood of anxiousness within management, because new brooms sweep clean, especially brooms new to the organisation. Geraint was no different. He wanted his own team around him, and he was rightly excited at the prospect of joining the BBC, shaping its future and putting his own stamp on the place. In many respects, he was following his father, Aneirin Talfan Davies, who followed Hywel Davies as head of programmes in the 1960s.

That summer of the interregnum was full of surprises and incidents. Ron Neill decided to visit us twice, in order to meet large gatherings of staff, when he proceeded to forecast a wonderful new dawn under the new leadership, at the same time denigrating the work of the *ancien régime*. It was his way of looking powerful. But my greatest pleasure came from observing at a distance the real power game of the early nineties. John Birt was Deputy Director General at that time, and he was about to pursue with the utmost zeal his goal of becoming the Director General. He left no stone unturned, not even Welsh ones. He had a holiday residence at Crickadarn, near Brecon, and, that summer he was a constant visitor. He attended a meeting of the Broadcasting Council in Cardiff; he came to the Royal Welsh Agricultural Show and the National Eisteddfod; and he invited a group of staff, including John Parry and me, to his house for a convivial supper. These unprecedented series of visits were intended, at best, to show an interest in Welsh affairs, but, in truth, the objective was to lobby the National Governor for his vote when the time came to select the next Director General, in a few months time. Predictably, it all went to plan.

Geraint arrived the first week of September and I decided my play-acting was done. At his first management meeting, I heard him announce, 'I don't like smoking. I don't approve of the club on the BBC site, and I dislike office politics.'

It was going to need a chief assistant to manage that little lot. It certainly was different. During the first week, he asked me to accompany him to see a firm of accountants. They were to act as consultants to BBC Wales, to pinpoint the way forward by making financial savings. Their initial report, which they produced in six weeks, was a blueprint for plunder. I decided then to leave well before Christmas, in fact, in the first week of November. It was the right time, and Geraint's farewell functions and luncheons for me were generous and warm. Whatever had been the irritations and the play-acting of the past months, I enjoyed those last few weeks. I wallowed in music with good friends. I accompanied the BBC Welsh Symphony Orchestra on two European concert tours.

We spent a memorable ten days in October, visiting Prague, Dresden, Leipzig and Berlin, and my last weekend as a BBC employee I spent in Paris. I had been involved with the Orchestra's music making for radio and television since my first days with *Children's Hour*. I had witnessed its development and growing 'band' of thirty players, until it attained full symphonic status, and had witnessed the fights to ensure adequate funding and status. I had worked with a succession of heads of music, from composers such as Arwel Hughes and Mansel Thomas, to Arnold Lewis, Merfyn Williams and Huw Tregelles Williams. The opening of St David's Hall in Cardiff was a landmark, providing a wonderful platform for radio and television concerts. International recognition came in the eighties with conductors Paavo Berglund, Mariss Jansons, Andrew Davis, Roger Norrington and Tadaaki Otaka, and the tours to Canada, the Soviet Union, Japan and Europe.

Huw Tregelles Williams had master-minded the Orchestra's expansion and nurtured its growing reputation. Under his leadership, BBC Wales became a television centre of excellence for music-making, from orchestral programmes such as the acclaimed series of Tchaikovsky symphonies, to recitals and concerts with singers Stuart Burrows, Denis O'Neill, Gwyneth Jones and Margaret Price. The partnership with the Welsh National Opera, and television relays of productions such as the Janáček season and the acclaimed Peter Stein production of *Falstaff* added to its prestige.

Listening to music was a fitting end to my time in broadcasting, and the journey to Eastern Europe was especially moving. The cold war had just ended, the beautiful city of Prague was reawakening, its people beginning to savour the first months of freedom from tyranny. The concert in Berlin marked the official celebrations of the re-unification of Germany when, a year earlier, its people from east and west had torn down the wall. In Paris, at the awe-inspiring Madeleine Church, where the composer Fauré had been organist, the Orchestra and Chorus – another innovation – marked the centenary of his birth with a performance of his *Requiem*, on a cold, sunny, Sunday afternoon. As the last notes were held before drifting upwards to the vaulted roof, the great west doors opened slowly, and the beams of the late-autumn sunshine lit the high altar. It was uplifting.

A long lunch orchestrated by John Stuart marked my last day. It was a splendid occasion, full of memories, laughter and tall stories. I would miss that, the kindness and support and the friendship. I went to visit Lorraine, now retired. She was lively and as direct as ever.

'Well, I've retired,' I said, not expecting any comment because I often went to see her.

She looked up from stirring two mugs of tea. 'God, you don't look old enough.'

Somehow, I felt my broadcasting life had come full circle. My working days were over.

More autobiographies from Y Lolfa that you will enjoy...

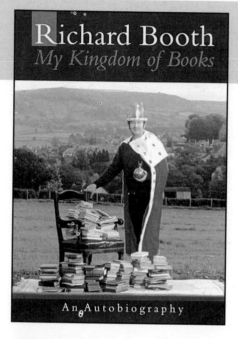

My Kingdom of Books

Richard Booth

The candid, anarchic autobiography of the colourful, eccentric second-hand book trader. Richard Booth recalls a lifetime searching the world for books, and his work in developing Hay-on-Wye as the second-hand book capital of the world.

£14.95

ISBN: 0 86243 495 5

Solva Blues

Meic Stevens

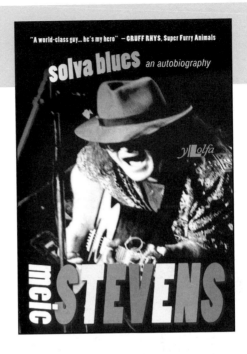

"A world-class guy... he's my hero" – GRUFF RHYS, Super Furry Animals

Solva blues *an autobiography*

y Lolfa

Meic STEVENS

The remarkable story of the acclaimed Welsh singer-song writer Meic Stevens, described as the UK's leading song-writer by none other than Bob Dylan.

Marvel at his incredible life told in his own words. Share his elation as he reaches the top with Warner Brothers, as well as his despair as he hits a bleak spiral of depression...

"A world-class guy... he's my hero."
Gruff Rhys, Super Furry Animals

"A riveting read and a fascinating insight into what made a musical genius tick." **Hefin Wyn**

£9.95

ISBN: 0 86243 732 6

The Green Casanova

Mike Bloxsome

Peter Freeman was a politician born in the East End of London – a vegetarian, animal rights activist, sports star, green campaigner and philanderer to boot. His parliamentary bill to ban fox hunting was introduced in 1929! A Brecon newspaper called him the 'Friend of the Lobster' after he had campaigned to ban the boiling of lobsters alive in the Commons kitchens. He had a reputation as a man with many 'women companions', yet this is a love story as unexpected as everything else about him.

"Peter Freeman emerges from this remarkable book as a brilliant humanitarian and devolutionist."
Rhodri Morgan, First Minister of the Welsh Assembly

£6.95

ISBN: 0 86243 7245